The Biographer's Gift

The Biographer's Gift

Life Histories and Humanism

Edited by
JAMES F. VENINGA

Published for the Texas Committee for the Humanities by
Texas A&M University Press
College Station

Library of Congress Cataloging in Publication Data
Main entry under title:

The Biographer's gift.

    Bibliography: p.
    Includes index.
    1. Biography (as a literary form—Addresses,
essays, lectures. I. Veninga, James F. (James Frank),
1944–
CT21.B46 1983   808'.06692   83-45093
ISBN 0-89096-168-9

Manufactured in the United States of America
FIRST EDITION

Contents

Preface

In recent decades biography has achieved unprecedented popularity. We have seen new and sometimes dramatic departures in the ancient art of telling lives. These departures have received nourishment from advances in the social sciences, especially psychology and sociology, but other disciplines, including literary criticism, have had their impact. These trends have not been without controversy, and fundamental questions about the nature and meaning of biography continue to be asked.

The 1982 Texas Lecture and Institute on the Humanities, sponsored by the Texas Committee for the Humanities, a state program of the National Endowment for the Humanities, sought to address these questions, to ascertain what biography is and is not, and to learn how the writer puts a biography together. Frank E. Vandiver, the 1982 Texas Lecturer on the Humanities, provided the keynote address, "Biography as an Agent of Humanism." Biographers Robert H. Abzug, Stephen B. Oates, Ronald Steel, and Jean Strouse responded to Vandiver's paper. Conversations with four of the five biographers, published first in the *Texas Humanist* (vol. 4, no. 4, 1982), are also included in this volume. These five authors have written twenty-two books, including full biographies of eight men and women.

In planning the Lecture and Institute, the Texas Committee for the Humanities expressed interest in the "uses" of biography and the insight gained through the reading of recounted lives. Steven Weiland's and my papers attempt to pursue this matter, the first by focusing on the implications of biography for understanding the professions and the second by clarifying the broader meaning of biography for the interested public. These endeavors reflect an important goal of the Lecture and Institute: to bring together not only biographers and persons with professional interest in biography but avid and critical readers—schoolteachers, physicians, ranchers, lawyers, business people, and others—who wished to explore the significance of biography.

The rise of interest in biography in recent decades parallels an important phenomenon of contemporary culture: the growing crisis of confidence in the institutions of society. As our institutions grow more distant, virtually impenetrable, and seemingly uncaring, our curiosity about how other people live and what they think and feel increases. We want to know the private lives of public people, and we want to know the lives of "common" men and women—people like ourselves—who have struggled with the possibilities and limitations of life. We respond to the impersonal nature of contemporary life with great curiosity about previous times and particular lives. Through biography we reach out to others to understand ourselves. In this age of Freud and his intellectual descendants we crave insight, if not wisdom, in the business of living.

In 1970, Richard Ellmann, in his inaugural lecture as Goldsmiths' Professor of English Literature at New College, Oxford University (*Literary Biography*, 1971), acknowledged that we want more from our biographies now than we did in the past. "More than anything else," he said, "we want in modern biography to see the character forming, its peculiarities taking shape."

One important result of this emphasis is that the modern biographer no longer feels many of the constraints that shaped the endeavors of his predecessors. Daniel Aaron, in the preface to the collection of essays *Studies in Biography* (1978), argues that, except for the possibility of libel or problems related to access of information, "the biographer today is virtually unrestricted." But Aaron also argues that "the old ethical questions . . . continue to assert themselves" and that new challenges emerge as well, for "the modern biographer's very freedom and the variety of his options create new methodological problems as well as new expectations on the part of the reader." These factors tend to make the biographer "dig deeper into such matters as parental influence, stages of growth, historical conditioning—to fix on certain illuminating occasions and to try to penetrate the veil of unconscious or calculated deceptions most people hang between themselves and the world."

The peculiar convergence at this time of old questions, new challenges, and increased expectations invites us to review the history of the biographical craft, to see afresh those twists and turns of artistic endeavor that have shaped the tradition. Especially there is need to sort through the fundamentals of biography to see what is enduring and what is truly new in the "New Biography." Richard Ellmann reminds us that, despite the current psychological drift of biography, one is still driven back to James Boswell's *Samuel Johnson* (1791) to understand the brilliance of good biography. "The greatness of Boswell's biography," writes Ellmann, "the sense it imparts of a man utterly recognizable and distinct, demonstrates that other methods of biography are not necessarily better." And Frank Vandiver notes in this volume that, however much biography may have changed, the biographer's goal remains "to evoke from the past the essence of a subject, the character that quickened blood and bone." Ideas on method, technique, tone, structure, and emphasis are as diverse as biographies published, but biography at its best, states Vandiver, "brings a touch of humanity from the past and can, if deftly done, offer a glimpse of humanity in microcosm."

For a civilization clouded by uncertainty, that, indeed, is a gift beyond measure.

JAMES F. VENINGA
Austin, Texas

Acknowledgments

The Texas Lecture and Institute on the Humanities is designed to highlight the work and thought of prominent Texans who have contributed to the humanistic tradition in American thought and literary activity. In establishing this series, the Texas Committee for the Humanities recognized that, in light of the increasing attention given in American society to science and technology, on the one hand, and to very practical concerns, on the other hand, there has been, in recent years, decreasing emphasis on the humanities in our elementary and secondary schools, in our colleges and universities, and in the private lives of our citizens. Hence this annual humanities program is rooted in the most basic objective of the Texas Committee for the Humanities: to foster public understanding and appreciation of the humanities. In his opening remarks at the Lecture, Roy M. Mersky, professor of Law and director of research at the University of Texas School of Law and chair of the Texas Committee for the Humanities in 1982, summarized the committee's goal in establishing this public humanities program: "By recognizing each year a Texan, or someone with roots in Texas, for extraordinary work in a discipline of the humanities, we honor all persons in Texas whose lives are dedicated to the humanities—public school teachers, liberal arts faculty members in our colleges and universities, writers and journalists."

A number of people made invaluable contributions toward the success of the 1982 Texas Lecture and Institute, and I take this opportunity to acknowledge their service.

My deepest gratitude is expressed to Edmund L. Pincoffs, former chair of the Texas Committee for the Humanities and professor of Philosophy at the University of Texas at Austin, whose life and thought exemplify the noble ideal of the public humanist, for first conceiving an annual Texas Lecture and Institute on the Humanities.

The program of 1982 would not have been successful without the able oversight of members of the planning subcommittee: Jesus Hinojosa, professor of Urban and Regional Planning at Texas A&M University; Konstantin Kolenda, McMannis Professor of Philosophy at Rice University; Roy Mersky; and George Woolfolk, professor of History at Prairie View A&M University.

Other members of the Texas Committee for the Humanities, past and present, made particular contributions in the program itself: Betty Anderson, past president of the Texas League of Women Voters; Jack Carlson, professor of History at Austin College; Carolyn Galerstein, dean of General Studies at the University of Texas at Dallas; Archie McDonald, a biographer and professor of History at Stephen F. Austin State University; Sandra Myres, professor of History at the University of Texas at Arlington; and Leila Smith, associate dean of Arts and Sciences at El Paso Community College. To Roy Mersky, who offered invaluable advice and who served effectively as moderator of the three-day program, special thanks is tendered.

Deep appreciation is extended to my fellow staff members for their professionalism and efficiency in planning and implementing the 1982 Lecture and Institute: Kim Hughey, Alison Paggi, Robert O'Connor, and, especially, Judy Diaz, whose eye for detail is second to none.

I also wish to thank Gaines Post, Jr., associate professor of History at the University of Texas at Austin and chair of the Publication Subcommittee of the Texas Committee for the Humanities, for his encouragement in publishing the papers of the 1982 Texas Lecture and Institute.

On behalf of the Texas Committee for the Humanities, I express appreciation to the Hoblitzelle Foundation, Dallas, and the Lola B. Wright Foundation, Austin, for their grants in support of the program of 1982 and to the National Endowment for the Humanities, which provided federal matching funds.

Finally, I express my gratitude to Frank Vandiver, the 1982 Texas Lecturer on the Humanities, for launching this annual program with elegant style, bold enthusiasm, and enticing imagination, and to his colleagues in biography who participated eloquently: Jean Strouse, Robert Abzug, Stephen Oates, and Ronald Steel.

J. F. V.

The Biographer's Gift

Biography as an Agent of Humanism

FRANK E. VANDIVER

How could biography be anything but an agent of humanism? The title of this address seems to be sufficient for the message. Yet there are too many meanings of both biography and humanism to justify an urge to avoid talking for a decent moment on a subject of tantalizing dimensions.

Biography as a literary genre has undergone a sea change in this century. From the ancients' moral lesson to Victorian elegiac to Freudian revelation to modern life re-creation—so runs the history of biography. But the roads to the present in life-writing are various, and the varieties confusing indeed.

Humanism, too, boasts a checkered history. By definition, humanism is a complex variable. According to the *Oxford English Dictionary*, humanism embraces "belief in the mere humanity of Christ," "any system of thought or action which is concerned with merely human interests (as distinguished from divine)," and also "devotion to those studies which promote human culture." By usage, "humanism" was the label given to the new study of Greek and Roman antiquities that sparked the Renaissance. Recently humanism has come to serve an especially malign purpose—as whipping boy for the New Right. Seizing on that part of the definition which speaks of "belief in the mere humanity of Christ," New Right demagogues seek to smear one of the finest scholarly traditions with their own conception of a horrid agnosticism. So humanism is certainly a useful term.

What, from all these possibilities, am I going to talk about? I propose to speak of art and empathy; I want to look at biography as an art form and at humanism as the "character of being human"—really as a special quality that quickens human clay.

One simile above all others recurs in writing about biography—the comparison of biographers with portraitists. From Plutarch to André Maurois to Barbara W. Tuchman biographers have remarked the kinship they feel with portrait painters. And the analogy is apt, for biography can range in scope from a sketch—a pencil outline—to a full, total account—a large canvas; and biography can be written in small segments—in light brushstrokes—or in a variety of layers—shadings—or even in overwhelming totality—say, the Hudson River treatment! Most important is that both forms of art aim at the same purpose: to illuminate reality.

All biographers know the need to build their subject's life through time and career, know the need to layer in details and traits as time shapes a nature. Pundits and popular psychologists speak glibly of "passages" in human lives; biographers would generally welcome so simple a solution to problems of maturation and change. They know all too well that formulas cannot substitute for facts, that personalities differ, that reactions stem from sources which refuse easy listing, and that people gleefully defy pigeonholes.

Biographers, because they have some perception of people, are a peculiar lot. In some ways they remind me of George Santayana's historian—as, at one and the same time, the highest and lowest of creatures. The historian fitted that definition because he would know so much about his subject that he would be inundated. "Such knowledge," said philosopher Santayana, "must dissolve thought in a vertigo if it has not already perished of boredom."

All biographers must steep themselves in data, work with those data for some time, let them work on them, and then begin to pick and choose what they perceive as necessary to shape a person from the past—more than that, to evoke a person into being.

Evocation of personality, of character, is the highest biographical art. Description, analysis even, can come without evocation, but when a person seems to come off the pages in full force, then the biographer has truly succeeded. That kind of witchery follows great familiarity with a subject's times and contemporaries, problems, travails, triumphs, loves, and losses. To achieve that kind of immersion, a biographer must live with a subject, in fact, must go back into time and a life and walk old footprints—walk in another's moccasins, in American Indian parlance.

All things that touched the subject—people, artifacts, papers, memoirs, oddments of costume, fancies, speeches, recordings, writings—are the biographer's clay. And they are not inert, these dry scripts and shards; they guide a writer's pen and often subdue a scholar's wish. Beyond the remains—beyond what I call the existential evidence—there is another layer of evidence that no biographer can ignore. This layer—which, for want of a better term, I call the "secondary evidence" (Leon Edel calls it the "psychological evidence")—constitutes the meanings, appreciations, nuances of character that can be deduced from the existential evidence and from traits and habits. Both layers are vital, both available only after hard research.

Evidence is, of course, the main ingredient in life-writing. But mere massing of data is no guarantee of evocation. Biographers have to provide the final human ingredient of translation. And as they study what they have discovered, as they ply the business of evocation, they must be on guard against external conditions that may warp their work.

Every discipline endures various fads—biography and history are no exceptions. As new ideas and techniques in science and social science developed, some historians and biographers tried to use them in penetrating the past. Especially has this been true with regard to science—in part, I think, because scientists have become the magicians of our time. Social science followed along as fast as possible, seeking to graft onto the great cornucopia in Washington. Among the new tools that appear especially useful to studies of people is, of course, psychology. Although psychology suffers cross doctrines and quarreling theories, historians and biographers have seized on it and plunged into analyses of hidden motives, disturbed libidos, unbalanced minds. Results have been mixed, at least to me. Sigmund Freud and William C. Bullitt wrote a psychological study of Woodrow Wilson that hardly charmed reviewers and, in fact, seemed to underscore a telling comment by Emile Durkheim to the effect that history could be used to elucidate psychology but never the reverse. Psychoanalysis can aid the biographer, but only when skillfully handled.

There is another facet of science that some biographers tie to—and that crosses psychoanalysis with biology. This branch of biography is sometimes called biopsychology or dynamic psychology and is well illustrated by Robert W. White's *Lives in Progress: A Study in the Natural Growth of Personality.* White's passion is to elucidate "natural growth of personality," that is, the development through time of nonaberrant psyches. His case studies make good reading and emphasize the biographer's need to portray a subject's growth and development, to paint a life in maturing stages of change.

Social science, too, charms biography. Sociology helps lifewriting, but not directly. So far, sociology tends to talk of societies, of large numbers, of groups rather than individuals. Economics toys with laws, and political science focuses on the behavior of voters and governments at various levels. Anthropology, by its very nature, broadens its lens to whole peoples in the past. Archaeology comes closet to history and biography in its impartial acceptance of artifacts left by one or by many.

In recent years all social sciences have been heavily influenced by psychology. Most of them are grouped under the umbrella name "behavioral sciences," since they study mass reaction and motivation. Some historians and biographers cherish the behaviorist label and would wave it proudly over their books and papers. But the main body of biography still clings to individuality, still seeks to know how one man or woman lived and worked in his or her time, how one life may have influenced many.

Lest I be accused of ignoring a rich contributory stream, let me mention a growing interest among some historians in group studies. Such outstanding scholars as George F. Rudé, with *The Crowd in History,* and Richard C. Cobb, with *Death in Paris* and *Paris and Its Provinces,* have extended the dimensions of group psychology and discovered a collective personality that promises new and greater insight into man.

And now there are whole categories of normally "silent" people emerging from obscurity because of recent approaches to research that shift biographical perception. I am referring to Richard Cobb's study of a single class of French workers—personal servants—whose opinions about their employers, their nation, and the world change what we know of pre-revolutionary Europe. These people are articulate now because new approaches to evidence lifted the cloak of obscurity and gave them life.

A new trend toward psychoanalytical biographies fogged in jargon is altogether dismal. Jargon has taken over much writing in the social sciences. Obscurantism marches on!

I have noticed an interesting contrast in historical or biographical works about science or scientists written by scientists. These studies are often models of clarity. Consider such recent works as Daniel J. Kevles's *The Physicists* or Elof Axel Carlson's *Hermann J. Muller*. Donald Clayton, a Rice space physicist, writes gracefully of the cosmos. So, too, does mathematician E. T. Bell, write fascinatingly about his colleagues, in *Men of Mathematics*. Isaac Asimov is perhaps the best-known science fictioner—and is no mean scientist. Precision is not the only hallmark of scientists as writers about their colleagues and their fields—they pull readers into their subjects with strong, muscular prose, and they tell good stories. At any rate, most of them avoid jargon.

Can the same be said of historians and biographers—do they write crisply of their kind and field? Large collective works on historiography lack literary distinction. James Thomson Shotwell's *History of History* is interesting but fairly typical collective biography—a book that assesses rather than evokes—and that is not a criticism, since Shotwell's aim is not to do biography but to analyze contributions made by various scholars. Michael Kraus's *History of American History* strikes me as more critical and less interesting than Shotwell's larger work.

Biographers have hacked away at their colleagues with gusto. Boswell has his Frederick Pottle, but in general biographers suffer from collective analysis or in essays done in dudgeon by collegial reviewers. A great many of them come to the surface for a line or two in how-to books on biography, usually examples of how-not-to! There is a healthy kind of jealousy abroad in the biographical world—the kind that spurs and spites and stimulates—and has, I think, elevated the genre.

A good deal of fine writing, though, has been done by biographers about biography. Like Leon Edel or not, he writes engagingly and with feeling about how to write another's life. I personally disagree with 98 percent of his well-selling *Literary Biography* but confess its charm and persuasion. André Maurois's *Aspects of Biography* suits my taste more happily, and here, again, is an artist limning his art. If I were asked my favorite work about biography, I would name instantly Paul Murray Kendall's *The Art of Biography*. There is nothing pious in it; it simply says more about a biographer's obligations and explains more about a biographer's problems in a few pages than can be found in countless tomes on writing. Kendall is a distinguished biographer. Experience lends an extra dimension to his discussion of research, technique, and evocation. Only one who has suffered the toils of wringing a human being from the mists could so well describe the value of seeing and knowing places that a subject walked or knew. Kendall has called Louis XI from long ago, has brought the "Spider King" to sparking life—and has done it because he lived with him, touched his bones, and walked in his swirling dust.

Kendall believes, as do Veronica Wedgwood and many others, that he must go where his subject went to share feelings and to know a personality. He says: "The interaction of biographer and subject is heightened by the biographer's direct, sensory experience of the matrix from which the subject's experience has been shaped. The biographer opens himself to all that places and things will tell him, in his struggle to visualize, and to sense, his man in being." Real knowledge of a subject demands more: "Deepest of all, the particular kind of biographer of whom I am speaking, cherishes, I believe a conviction—call it a romantic quirk, if you will—that where the subject has trod he must tread, what the subject has seen he must see, because he thus achieves an indefinable but unmistakable kinship with his man." In personal terms, Kendall confesses that "it would be vain for me to assert that the biography of Louis XI . . . will be demonstrably abler because I have held in my hand—within the whispering vault by Cléry, the church he built—the massive skull which still, by the language of sheer bone, bespeaks the marvelously ugly countenance of that consummate actor." He believes, though, that places do tell things to biographers. He says that on a visit to Louis's battlefield at Montlhéry, where the king waged, "under circumstances which dramatically reveal the motions of his character, a wild, bloody battle with his mortal foe, Charles of Burgundy, I believe that I learned more than the physical appearance of terrain and the probable movements of the armies." And the sight of the field on a July day much like the one of battle made an impression to carry beyond the moment into art:

There stood fields of wheat and beans shimmering in the sun, there lay the village canted on the hillside, and at my back, gray stone walls of the royal castle. Perhaps I am deceived in thinking that what then happened to me was more than a *frisson*, a literary thrill. I can but report that I felt a shock of recognition, a poignant apprehension of Louis that I had not previously achieved.

What will happen to works such as Kendall's, works in the literary tradition, if science and pseudoscience lock hold on biography? They will vanish in a mass of statistics, in a maze of models and computer printouts. That thought brings a dismal image of a day when books are themselves artifacts, all reading is done on consoles, and biography is offered by regression analysis and probability theory.

Of course, by now you know that I like literary biography—if not in the Edel sense! It is, I know, often criticized as old-fashioned, as a throwback to Lytton Strachey, even to Suetonius and Plutarch. Modern practitioners like Edel, and many in the psychological school, argue that literary biographies lack new perceptions and depths and are tied too closely to imagination. These allegations are partly true and partly false. Biography as literature has really come into its own in this century. Strachey blew open the genre with *Eminent Victorians*, followed by his artful *Life of Queen Victoria*. Clearly style and content could mix, and biography could be stimulating social history as well as life simulation. All kinds of avenues were tried, from a new kind of autobiographical approach that accepted fiction within its confines (Robert Graves's *I, Claudius* is a fine example) to the openly fictionalized life (Catherine Drinker Bowen's *Yankee from Olympus* ranks at the top).

Scholarly biography, long viewed askance by readers and publishers, had caught a large segment of the popular market by the mid-1950s. Although Albert J. Beveridge's *John C. Marshall* (1916–19) had long loomed over American biography, it seemed more a landmark than a beacon. It was the happy blend of subject and biographer that opened the way for scholarly writers to take honorable place at biography's table. An editor at Scribner's decided in the early 1920s that the market might stand a one-volume life of Robert E. Lee. He asked a young Virginian, Douglas Southall Freeman, to write it. Freeman had published a large collection of Lee letters and had gained wide renown as a rising scholar at Johns Hopkins University. Freeman worked for almost twenty years and produced four large volumes. Despite its bulk, despite the frighteningly careful research reflected in an awesome array of footnotes, *R. E. Lee: A Biography* immediately set new standards for literature, scholarship, and biography. It stands as a perennial model for biographies.

Freeman's background—his own biography—lent strength to his work. A newspaperman, he wrote daily, knew how to find facts and how to use them. Residence in Richmond gave him an entree to sources kept for the faithful, and his own upbringing etched the value of character. Lee emerged from Freeman's pages a graceful, gentle man with a romance running deep in the blood––a romance that could rage and make a tall, courtly soldier a fiery man of war. What Freeman brought to his task proved vital.

Other examples of modern biographical literature

abound. Stephen Oates, present here, writes as I would like to write. The late T. Harry Williams, famed for his *Huey Long*, wrote with equal grace and perhaps even deeper understanding in *Lincoln and His Generals*. Confederate general P. G. T. Beauregard also caught his attention, and *Napoleon in Gray* is still the best on the subject. Williams is worth more consideration—he wrote two kinds of biography—of one and of many. And he did both with gusto. Research was a hallmark, but style was his forte. His books will linger as primers of organization, method, and presentation.

Sinclair Lewis, that prodigious literary force, has attracted one of the best biographies of our age—the massive study by Mark Schorer. I confess to having had only a slight interest in Lewis, but once beyond the title page of Schorer's book, I was caught—caught as much by the biography as by the subject. So artful, insightful, so crafted are Schorer's pages that they pull the reader into Lewis's life, ready or not. That kind of biography poses, I think, a fascinating question: How true to life is it? Is the subject made by the book? It can happen, of course—a book can drag its theme to greatness. In biography, however, that kind of alchemy, it seems to me, is dangerous. Not that I think that the subject should overwhelm the biographer—far from it. I do think, though, that a subject should command respect, admiration, or total damnation on his or her own merits. Cast to the future in false dimension may sometimes seem a happy prospect, but not really. A man or woman deserves his or her own size and merits, and biographers have an obligation not to distort, willfully or otherwise.

That demand for dimensional accuracy hampers biographers' imagination and, in some ways, levies a harsher burden than even historians carry. Both biographers and historians honor facts; biographers honor, too, personality and character and must do no violence to either.

In their quest for responsible accuracy, life-writers now deploy far more tools for rummaging in the past than ever before. Science, of course, aids, abets, and sometimes curses, along with social science. New dimensions of social history often help us see a subject in proper surroundings. Art, music, theater—each offers a glimpse at interests, perhaps even motivation.

In the reaches of mass biography, history touches closely—and the touch seems to reinforce the old assertion that biography is the handmaiden of history. Barbara W. Tuchman, in a graceful essay entitled "Biography as a Prism of History," says that, as a prism, biography "attracts and holds the reader's interest in the larger subject. People are interested in other people, in the fortunes of the individual." Biography is also attractive, Tuchman thinks, "because it encompasses the universal in the particular. It is a focus that allows both the writer to narrow his field to manageable dimensions and the reader to more easily comprehend the subject. . . . the artist, as Robert Frost once said, needs only a sample. One does not try for the whole but for what is truthfully *representative*."

To my mind collective biography is one of the most difficult and useful branches of the life-writing art. Tuchman uses it skillfully in her wide-ranging histories; historians often use the biographical sketch to highlight an age with a person. There have been, and are, biographers who offer whole sets of sketches as the best avenue to understanding people, place, and time. Plutarch's *Parallel Lives* were deftly honed to intrigue readers while teaching them ethics. Writing, though, ranked high with Plutarch. He knew the value of attracting an audience. His sketches still read well, and the ethics intrude little enough as lives parade from an ancient world. Gamaliel Bradford's "psychographs" added attraction to the field as they followed Strachey's new wave. Bradford's work I find useful yet; his *Union Portraits* and *Confederate Portraits* show his knack of quick evocation—a style and art worth continuing. Hendrik Willem Van Loon's *Lives* is another venture into the sketcher's realm—again, the results are intriguing and set character and person easily in time and place.

I have saved Strachey's *Eminent Victorians* for a special word. Graceful, "lacquered" style, skilled insights, willingness to shake traditions willy-nilly, sometimes scalding wit, all contained in Strachey's work, set new directions for life-writing.

He broke idols. Biography had, in his time, languished in a kind of filiopietistic moralism that inundated readers in undigested facts interlined with preachy praise of the subject. Hardly an art, biography survived simply because it still boasted people for its topic.

Strachey boasted people when he thought it right. He damned them when they deserved damning, and he damned his biographical colleagues who strung facts together without a care for art. Large, two-volume lives he hated: "They are as familiar as the *cortège* of the undertaker, and wear the same air of slow, funeral barbarism." For him these granite tomes taught lessons: "To preserve . . . a becoming brevity—a brevity which excludes everything that is redundant and nothing that is significant. . . . To maintain his (the biographer's) own freedom of spirit. It is not his business to be complimentary, it is his business to lay bare the facts of the case as he understands them."

Strachey's iconoclasm brought respectability to life-writing and ushered in human foibles as legitimate concerns. His work did much for the sketchers, who could at last limn their subjects as people, not as icons. The eminent Victorians who throng Strachey's pages show sketching as a higher art. Not long, the sketches are nimble, graceful, witty, and caustic, and they charm because they persuade. From that model stem the many clusters of lives I have mentioned before.

There is another cachet approach in biography: the dictionary school. Dictionaries are not new; they have enjoyed scholarly gratitude for more than a century. *Larousse, The Dictionary of National Biography, Appleton's*—these are traditionals. Of them all I think that *The Dictionary of American Biography* sets an unmatched tone of style and content. First under the guidance of Dumas Malone, an eminent biographer of Jefferson, then under John A. Garraty, this distinguished series continues to raise new standards. And who is to argue that there is not more useful history in such a compilation than in all the history books? At least, with my prejudices, I find history there especially palatable.

Which leads back to the matter of biography as a handmaiden of history. I would argue that both are handmaidens of each other. Whether or not you agree with Thomas Carlyle and the "great man" theory of history, you must concede that people do make history. People even shape some of the so-called great forces that seem immutable—economics, for example.

I am intrigued by the part that human reactions play in shaping history—especially human accommodation to events over which people have no control. Acts of God demand man's response: great storms that kill thousands bring human palliation; shifting ground and sweeping plagues produce reactions that, in themselves, create history. These reactions deserve more biographical magnification.

In my own particular area, military history, biography is unusually important—and I would really like to call myself a military biographer rather than a military historian. I say that biography is important in the study of military affairs because the careers of great captains do loom above the mass of lives—and in the careers of these men can often be glimpsed lessons for younger leaders. Why? Because the art of war resembles other arts—techniques and practices, skills and applications vary in various hands, but the true artist creates personal rules.

Biography is important, too, in the military realm because it forces concentration on specific human qualities instead of on operations, intelligence, logistics, training—all the details of war administration. All great philosophers and commentators on war have remarked on a trait that is shared by great captains, one trait that separates the true leader from other ranks: character. Definitions of the quality vary, yet there is general acceptance of some elements common to superior battle commanders. Physical courage they all share, a touch of fatalism, too, that lends deliberateness to their deeds, and most of all a way of sticking, a firmness not given to many as battles shift and sway, a sense of purpose and resolve that carries out to their soldiers and creates optimism. Commentators from the ancient Chinese Sun Tzu to General Maxwell Taylor remark the need for character. If they all perceive it differently, they all concede its grace. Great captains who have it are not always the bravest, not always the glorious—but they have an honesty bred that gives trust in their orders and faith in their plans. Character, that elusive mark of honor, is the luminous hallmark of great soldiers from Miltiades to Douglas MacArthur.

What is it about character that so entices admiration? It is, for one thing, the quality that seems to sift the few from the rest. Those who stand the test of truth and perseverance are celebrated—witness Winston Churchill on Marlborough, virtually hundreds on Napoleon, Freeman on Lee, John Wheeler-Bennett on Hindenburg, Anthony Nutting on T. E. Lawrence, Forrest C. Pogue on George C. Marshall. Character is often revealed in war reminiscences—those specialities of autobiography most artfully contributed by beaten commanders. The good ones show their strength of will, their devotion to victory, their dedication to the right course; bad ones reveal weakness through convenient memories and quick resort to blame.

Biographers lucky enough to live for some time in the company of a character sense a change in their own lives. I noted with pleasure Stephen Oates's remark that "I may have re-created Martin Luther King's life, but he changed mine." I share that feeling after five years' companionship with Stonewall Jackson and an eighteen years' trek after Black Jack Pershing.

Is human character an essential ingredient in history? I think so. And, if that is so, are biography and history separable?

They are separable, I think, only in the minds of students of the "laws of history," those scholars who put people at the bottom of the historical spectrum. The two fields are interdependent. In the works of Edward Gibbon and Michael I. Rostovtzeff, Thomas Carlyle and Lytton Strachey, Arnold Toynbee and Alexander Solzhenitsyn, Romain Rolland and Sir Winston Churchill, the genres blend.

Even though they blend, more readers flock to lives than to histories. Why? There is the obvious answer: People like to read about people. But is there something more, some intangible quality in written lives that attracts? Let me speak in my own terms about the biographer's business to see whether a discussion of the nature of the craft may reveal some hidden lure.

I think that biography—and I use the word to mean a study of someone no longer alive—is history made personal. Good biographies deal with the ways people faced living— tell how they met problems, how they coped with big and little crises, how they loved, competed, did the things we all do daily—and hence these studies touch familiar chords in readers.

Modern research techniques lend some new attractions to biography. As scholars use new tools to probe the past, even to plumb psyches, a multidimensional figure emerges from the sources. Social history perhaps adds an especially appealing facet to life-writing by the perspective it throws on the times of lives. Computer analysis can make easier the counting of monies and votes and even give a hint at probabilities—if the biographer dares to take the hint. Tape recorders offer recollections of a subject's contemporaries.

These new tools are added to the old and simply enlarge the biographer's sternest test—to select, arrange, organize the mass of data and conjure life from leavings. Here is where the "art" of the writer is tested: How witch from disparate sources not only the shape but also the actions of a subject and simulate a person? Whether or not a living being walks off the pages depends wholly on the biographer's skill as artist, conjurer, creator.

If evocation happens, it happens not by magic or by mirrors but by hard work. The biographer must live with a subject until he or she becomes real, until the writer shares a life. The result will not be a memoir, no matter how real the subject may seem, for the veil of existence cannot be broken, but it will be a study touched with empathy. I am convinced that no honest biographer—as opposed to the propagandist or the avowed debunker—can long remain in company and consort with a subject and avoid at least a touch of empathy.

Empathy is biography's quintessential quality—without

it lives are mere chronicles. It is the biographer's spark of creation.

Even with that spark the life-writer's choices of method are formidable. There are writers who believe that they can wander around in their subject's life, put in scenes from different times, scramble sentences, and generally rummage at will. Leon Edel speaks their case: "The biographer may be as imaginative as he pleases—the more imaginative the better—in the way in which he brings together his materials. . . . He may shuttle backward and forward in a given life; he may seek to disengage scenes or utilize trivial incidents . . . to illuminate character; he has so saturated himself with his documents that he may cut himself free from their bondage without cutting himself free from their truth." To me this kind of freedom is license and takes the biographer into the realm of fiction. A writer has an obligation, I think, to be innovative and original in research but to be careful to do no violence to a subject's development—and consequently not to tamper with sequence. A writer, too, must guard against distorting a subject's passions, problems, or pleasures.

Above all, I believe, a biographer must not assume knowledge of a subject's future. Edel screams in agony: "When I pick up a biography, I know before I open the book that it is the life of a statesman. . . . Our point of departure in the reading of a biography is not necessarily in the cradle, but with the man who achieved greatness." I side with André Maurois, who thinks that Edel "wants us to play a rather curious game of make-believe." Paul Murray Kendall agrees that all readers engage in make-believe as they begin a biography—they know that Woodrow Wilson became president, but they do not usually worry about his future as they trace him through childhood and early career. We know that we are the sum of our experience; we expect to follow a written life as it grows. How else can a life be simulated? Artists really do not ignore logic—they may conceive a new logic, but they follow its boundaries. Biographers do not have the luxury of tinkering; their subject's life is their logic. Straying produces untruth.

Another pitfall the biographer must avoid is that of

overidentification with a subject—superimposition, if you will, of the writer on the life being simulated. This is a real problem in modern life-writing, because life simulation involves reexperiencing the past with a subject. From this coexistence can come an almost unnoticed familiarity, a feeling that you—the writer—know your subject so well that you can predict reactions, feelings, jealousies—that you two think alike. Here the veil of existence seems nearly breached. How easy it would be to speak a subject's mind, and how specious! Years of acquaintance with your friends may lead you to a general sense of their feelings, but would you dare guess a friend's inner beliefs if they were never told to you? When your spouse enters the voting booth, are you absolutely sure?

How dare a biographer assume a thought, a bias, a prejudice of a subject unless some letter, some speech, some reliable source speaks? Freeman, who lived with General Lee for nearly twenty years, confessed that he never knew what was in Lee's mind unless he found the thought expressed somewhere. I lived with John Pershing for eighteen years and came to feel some friendship with him. I do not know to this day what his thoughts were—only what he said some of them were. To me the biographer's most forbidden ground is personal assumption. Of a subject's thoughts or beliefs nothing can be assumed.

I am not arguing that some things may not be taken as givens, that a writer may not use familiar things without racing for a footnote. All historians strive for verisimilitude, and one of the best ways to achieve it is to mix the sounds and sights of a place with action. This kind of art is at its best lost in its craft. Garrett Mattingly's classic *The Armada* is a good case study. He may assume, and use without fear of critic's horror, the sounds of the sea and ships, the sounds of wind and sail, the smells of powder and cordage. Freeman may loose the iron clangor of Gettysburg, the cries of charging, dying soldiers, for these are facts of his war. T. Harry Williams may rely on Louisiana's summer heat to shape one of Huey Long's harangues—and both writer and speaker show the impact of place. All these devices will be true to subject and circumstance—hence to art.

All other considerations aside, the biographer's goal is to evoke from the past the essence of a subject, the character that quickened blood and bone. It is the biographer's job to offer a subject to posterity—and that is no small responsibility. For that reason I think that the biographer's fundamental obligation is to understand—understand in all dimensions of the word.

For me, nothing is more necessary to the evocation of a life than full understanding of the person. More than that, I think that it is vital to understand a subject with sympathy and perhaps even to share viewpoints and ideas. I confess that this can be carried too far. Possibilities of oversympathizing hit me when I was working on my life of Stonewall Jackson. In the middle of a letter from General James Longstreet to Lee I struck a paragraph critical of Jackson and took it personally! That did seem to be a bit much. But in retrospect I was glad to realize that empathy had happened.

Similarly, when I became irritated with General Leonard Wood, I realized that part of me had reached some meeting ground with Pershing's prejudices. Lately I have started a Life of Field Marshal Douglas Haig, commander of the British armies in France during World War I. He is controversial, engages hot enmity from many studies as the consummate butcher in a butcher's war. I began with that impression, but after some time in his company, I feel pressures and considerations that negate any label. Empathy is happening. I have glimmers of what I hope is understanding.

Understanding can come in various ways. Experience can aid the biographer in evaluating evidence. This idea came recently, as I thought about a life of Jefferson Davis that I would like to write someday. The book would be far different from the one I would have written four or five years ago. A tour of duty in university higher administration has given me new perspective on Davis as Confederate president. Crosscurrents of constituencies, administrative pressures, the iron grip of money—all are parts of Davis's life. I simply would not have appreciated them had I written earlier. I could not have achieved understanding, much less empathy.

Empathy is a quality, I believe, that gives biography an

edge in attraction. A book that welds reader to subject commits a special kind of act: it offers a touch of friendship.

That touch is one of the reasons why biography is so much an agent of humanism. At its best, biography brings a touch of humanity from the past and can, if deftly done, offer a glimpse of humanity in microcosm.

There is an important connection between a biographer and a subject—the impact of one humanity on another. The good biographies really offer a special blend of two people, two humanities, a dual view of the human condition. Interestingly enough, both humanities focus on the same time, one as present, one as past, and provide almost stereoscopic perception.

As the biographer relives the past through the subject, so the subject evokes the past and serves the present. There is, in this unique relationship, part of the human continuum. "Never," says Jean Paul Richter, "does a man portray his own character more vividly, than in his manner of portraying another."

Times and things and thoughts change; ideas, fetishes, prejudices shift, but the interaction between biographer and subject still fascinates—and proves that one age can, through the art of biography, understand another, can touch and be understood—and hence can persist.

That persistence is the finest essence of humanism.

Responses

ROBERT H. ABZUG

In thinking about Frank Vandiver's remarks, I was struck by the way one question lurked behind every sentence and paragraph: What is the "witchery," as he called it, that makes the subjects of successful biographies "come off the pages in full force"? Searching for an answer, he endorsed or rejected various models and approaches and wisely gave us a kaleidoscope of possibilities rather than one definitive solution. I disagree with him on a number of points, including those concerning psychoanalysis and the fidelity to strict chronological sequence, but I remain intrigued by his central question. Wherein lies the magic? In search of the magic, I will in these remarks take a brief excursion into some of our differences but, I hope, will also contribute to our understanding of that "witchery" that makes good biography work.

I wish to explore beginnings. "Men can do nothing," wrote George Eliot, "without the make-believe of a beginning." Eliot's epigraph carries profound meaning for biography. It speaks to the necessity of a starting point and therefore of narrative itself, but also to the "make-believe" of identifying any particular moment as "first." Where does a life begin? Where, rather, does understanding a life begin? In ancestry? In a personal quirk? In birth, when all seems a clean slate, or in death, when only certain versions of a whole life have been etched out of the anarchy of experience? "No retrospect will take us to the true beginning," Eliot added. And yet the biographer must choose a starting point, because without the make-believe of a beginning he or she can do nothing.

Beginnings carry meanings. No wonder the importance of creation myths. Do you believe in the Big Bang or in Genesis? Each commences a radically different tale of the universe. How do you tell the story of a king? Do you begin with a long recitation of lineage, as in oral tradition or genealogy, or do you plunge into his affair with this or that mistress? At the least, each suggests a very different view of royalty and of society.

For modern biography the issues may not necessarily be so cosmic. As a biographer you do not create heavens and earth, but merely a life. However, you do not only birth a subject; you prefigure in some way the shape or essence of that life. And in those first pages, it seems to me, the biographer either captures or loses the reader depending upon the chemistry of that prefiguration.

That at least was the premise of my little experiment whose goal was to locate the "witchery" that captures readers. The experiment was simple. I took a pile of biographies that I happened to have around the house, ones that I liked, and began at the beginning. Rather than read them strictly for style or content, I let the Geiger counter in my mind tell me at what point I felt hooked. What irradiated passages made me read on? By isolating those moments, I hoped to learn more about the magic.

I turned first to Leon Edel's *Henry James: The Untried Years*, to that first page with which the author hoped to entice his reader into five volumes of prose. Edel opens in a confusion of names, noting that generations of Jameses had dubbed their sons either William or Henry, that the "names had become dynastic symbols, as if the family were a royal line and there was a throne to be filled." Edel continues:

Henry James the novelist and grandson of the enterprising William who had fared across the seas, was to plead often against the confusing proliferation of Williams and Henrys; and doubtless his passion for finding the right names for his fictional characters stemmed from a sense that wrong names had been bestowed within his family experience. It was difficult to be an individual if one's name were a family tag pinned to the cradles of helpless babes.

My mind's adrenalin began to surge. I saw Henry James in a sea of names, hacking out his life and prose as he swam to shore. Not yet born but already writing, he came alive for me in a timeless struggle revealed at that "make-believe" moment of starting.

Naturally I moved on to Jean Strouse's *Alice James*. The reciter of oral tradition would have given the brother and sister the same account of familial lines. Edel had culled a striking truth that linked Henry's psyche to his fiction. Strouse began differently, with a more personal intrusion into the chant of ancestry, one that made Alice James enter the book in force:

In 1890 (Alice was forty-two), one of Alice's cousins told her that the Robertson descent could be traced back to Robert Bruce, King of Scotland. "I asked how," retorted Alice. "Oh, why Robert*son*, son of Robert—er, er—Bruce!" "She showed me the coat-of-arms, but whether it was of the house of Robertson, Bruce, or Er—er, I couldn't clearly make out."

The dour, crusty, but somehow refreshingly straight-shooting Alice peered out amidst the strands of lineage. And a short chapter later I marveled at Strouse's echo of Edel: "Alice was the only one of the five James children not named for a relative or family friend. . . . In her childhood and adolescence, Alice was singular." An echo with a difference. From these passages on, I was intrigued by this solitary, unmarked James and her fate.

The prefiguring, the double image of the adult intruding into its own beginnings or even prehistory, was part of what appealed to me. It brought the promise of coherence even before I must face the anarchy of a person's life. Ronald Steel brought me this security in the beginning by suggesting the vulnerability of a precociously adult Walter Lippmann. Steel describes him as being shaken, at age eight, by the presence of Theodore Roosevelt. That brief image lived with me as Lippmann courted both the friendship and the confidence of great leaders and the love of his best friend's wife. And Stephen B. Oates, more mysteriously, reveals the presence of the Lincoln we know later, even as he sketches a fairly flat picture of young Lincoln, by describing "his thin, dark-haired mother, her eyes like pools of sadness." Those eyes carried me to the eyes of Lincoln during the Civil War, the craggy sadness that mirrored his greatness. In a simple description the book had been foreshadowed.

And I found myself moved by a book that began in shadow. In Justin Kaplan's *Walt Whitman* the reader meets the poet in his decline and death. I did not have to go beyond the first line to know that I would read on: "In the spring of 1884 the poet Walt Whitman bought a house in the unlovely city of Camden, New Jersey, and at the age of sixty-five slept under his own roof for the first time in his life." In an instant Kaplan crystallized all that I had known about Whitman the mythic wanderer and promised to tell me the sometimes unlovely but nonetheless more human truth. I was taken in again when Kaplan, having buried Whitman in the second chapter, moved me back to his chronological beginnings by quoting from the poet's "Facing West from California's Shores":

> But where is what I started for, so long ago?
> And why is it yet unfound?

The limits of time ended my search, but I thought that I had found at least a fragment of some personal truth about why some biographies worked. It seemed that the use of a particular technique or fidelity to narrative sequence or the cleaving to one or another social or behavioral science mattered little. Among the books I perused were those more or less enamored of psychoanalysis, more or less attached to straight chronology, more or less free in the terms of Leon Edel, more or less guilty of licentious tinkering in the court of Frank Vandiver.

What made these beginnings successful was less easily classifiable. In each case the author had made me feel at once the presence of the core of his or her subject and the illusion that that subject was yet to be created. The author had also identified a particular struggle, emotion, or myth connected with the subject that I felt duty-bound to watch elaborated.

In a sense each biographer had created the old Calvinist

drama, the struggle between free will and predestination. The universe of the biography became one in which the presupposition of a fate had been reinforced by prefiguring and foreshadowing intrusions, images, and the like; yet the expectation of a life to be relived, with all its turns and accidents, had not been destroyed. Indeed, it had been made more compelling. In this way, at least, good biography worked for me when it hinted in some quiet way that even as it assayed one life it ritually enacted every life.

RONALD STEEL

A biography is more than a factual account of a person's life. This statement seems obvious, and yet it is worth underlining, for the involvement of the biographer himself in the story is often ignored. A biography is a creative work, an amalgam of the life of the subject and the mind of the biographer.

"Philosophies are the very soul of the philosopher projected," the young Walter Lippmann once wrote of John Dewey. "A man's philosophy is his autobiography. You may read in it the story of his conflict with life." The way a person views the world, in other words, determines how he lives his life.

That seems a truism. Yet we can also turn it around and find it equally true. A person's autobiography is his philosophy. The way in which we live our lives reveals how we view the world.

In this sense biography—and also autobiography, for it is very much the same thing—has two facets. First, biography reveals how we deal with the world. It is the chronicle of events, of our actions. Second, it is a reflection of the prevalent belief system of the society in which we live. That is to say, a biography is phrased in terms of what society values.

What, in fact, does society value? That changes from time to time, from one period to another. But we know what our own society values. It teaches us to be concerned with the way in which people adjust to the outside world. We see this as more important than the way in which we are able to affect reality. The reason for this, of course, is clear: We live in a time when we feel that we have very little ability to shape fundamental realities.

Further, biography today is concerned more with describing the internal tensions experienced by an individual than with describing how an individual ought to live. In earlier periods biography focused on exemplary beings. It chronicled the lives of the saints, whether religious saints like Theresa or secular ones like Lincoln. But today we cannot write an account of an exemplary life because we are not sure what such a life is. We live in a time when social values, even moral values, are in flux. There is thus no consensus on what constitutes an exemplary life.

Biography may be an agent of humanism, but it also reflects a culture's values. We respond to the kind of biography—to the account of a person's conflict with life—that confirms the values we hold. And those values are, of course, transmitted to us through our culture. Our culture teaches us that the human being matters. It teaches us that a person should be in harmony with the system of values prescribed by his culture.

Fidelity to those values may, to be sure, place one at odds with society. The demands of the state are often not identical to the cultural values of society. In that case we will admire an individual who puts himself in conflict with the state, or with the pressure of his peers, in order to remain true to deeper cultural values.

Thus in our society we seek not reassuring tales of people who conform to society's restrictions but inspiring accounts of those who overcome obstacle and tradition. We are exalted not by lives of the saints but by heroic exploits against great odds and unfeeling bureaucracies. It matters to us less whether the indiviudal is triumphant than whether he has struggled nobly and remained true to his principles. In fact, we need not even admire the principles, as long as they are held with sufficient courage and determination.

Frank Vandiver has spoken of the careers of great captains as providing lessons for younger leaders. This has certainly been a theme of biography, and one of the reasons why it is so often taught in schools. But taken to an extreme, such an approach could reduce the biographer's task to that of a publicist or hagiographer. As a lesson provider he would be simply selling a product, emphasizing its good qualities and glossing over its blemishes so that readers would be impressed by the product's quality.

But this is only a partial view. Biographers today are not much interested in selling their subject as a paragon of virtue who will inspire the young. Rather, what concerns them is the way in which a human being grapples with society and with the contradictions of his own character. The result may be an exemplary figure, but often not. A protagonist need not be a hero. He can also be an anti-hero. Each is equally interesting, each important. An anti-hero is no less worthy a subject for biography than a hero—particularly at a time when there are no clear definitions of what makes a hero.

Mr. Vandiver has also stated that the biographer should avoid the superimposition of himself upon the subject. The forbidden ground for a biographer, he states, is personal assumption. I question whether the avoidance of superimposition or of personal assumption is possible. I also wonder whether it is desirable.

On the former count, it is, I believe, impossible for the biographer to avoid superimposing himself on the subject, not because of his failings as a biographer but because of his qualities as a human being. There is no way in which we can perceive another person, or even an object such as a bridge or painting, except by imposing that object on our psyche.

Even the most neutral description of a person, let alone a place or an object, is filtered through our conscious and subconscious. Each of us sees an object, and certainly a human being, differently, for each brings a different history and a different set of assumptions to what he sees. To a city dweller a fire hydrant will evoke images of water; to a desert nomad it might suggest a totem. Clearly, in one way or another, often without realizing it, we impose ourselves on what we see. How much more this is true when it concerns the actions of other human beings whom we are trying to interpret.

Biography is not the assembling of a jigsaw puzzle—with each piece filling one spot only and the ultimate design predetermined. Rather it is the creation (re-creation if you will) of a human character. In that act of re-creation the biographer inevitably imposes his values, the values of his culture, upon the character he is interpreting.

He may not do this willingly or even consciously. He can struggle against it. But he can never fully escape interpretation, even "superimposition," because it is inherent in the act of perception. The external world surely exists. But how it is described depends upon the individual perceptions of the person who is describing it.

In this sense one can truly say that biography is also autobiography. This link should be taken not so much literally as suggestively. The biographer is not an accountant or a résumé writer. He is an interpreter—a portrait painter, if you will. He is interested not in a photographic likeness, whatever that may be, but in psychological truth. Thus, like a painter or a sculptor, he must highlight certain qualities and diminish others. But what he chooses to emphasize is dictated by his perception of the character. He can have no other guide, for there is in truth no objective "reality" other than certain statistical facts. Everything else is interpretation.

The biographer must, as Frank Vandiver says, bring empathy to his task. He must also bring respect for the subject, as the subject saw himself—whether or not that subject is personally appealing to the biographer. But ultimately he must bring his creative imagination into play. There must be an imaginative leap into the unknown to capture the psychological reality underlying the statistical "facts." This leap into the unknown is the element that the greatest biographies share with fiction. What separates them from fiction is that they operate within an objective reality that must be respected.

"Once you touch the biographies of human beings," Walter Lippmann once wrote, "the notion that political beliefs are logically determined collapses like a pricked balloon." One might also say that once you touch the complex reality of human beings the notion that biographies are logically determined also collapses.

STEPHEN B. OATES

I applaud Frank Vandiver's wondrous ode to biography as literature and an agent of understanding humanity. I too submit that the best biography—true biography—remains a storytelling art whose mission, in the words of Paul Murray Kendall, is to elicit from the coldness of fact "the warmth of a life being lived." This is an old and honorable approach too often disparaged in a time that celebrates analysis and critical detachment in nonfiction. Not that true biography lacks analysis. Virtually everything said in good life-writing is the result of painstaking research, selection, and study. When it comes to composition, though, true biography is not critical analysis, is not an explanation of lifeless data and impersonal force, is not an author-dominated lecture in which the biographer pompously upstages his own subject, but is a form of literature that conveys the immediacy and reality of a life. It belongs to what Barbara W. Tuchman has termed "the literature of actuality."

Although Mr. Vandiver asserts that biography has changed radically in the last century, the stated aims of true life-writing—as Justin Kaplan has pointed out—have remained remarkably consistent from James Boswell in the eighteenth century to biographers in our own time. Said Boswell on his life of Samuel Johnson, "It appears to me that mine is the best plan of biography that can be conceived; for my readers will, as near as may be, accompany Johnson in his progress, and as it were, see each scene as it happened." Said Kendall, "The biographer's mission is to perpetuate a man as he was in the days he lived—a spring task of bringing to life again." Said Justin Kaplan: "Some believe, as I do, that the biographer is essentially a storyteller and dramatist—Henri Troyat's superb *Tolstoy* is much to the point here—and that a strong case should be made for enlarging the term 'literary biography' to include books that have literary qualities and not necessarily literary subjects."

Our difficulty today is that critics, far too many of them, do not regard biography as a distinct province of literature. As Leon Edel has complained: "I know of no critics in modern times who have chosen to deal with biography as one deals with poetry or the novel. The critics fall into the easy trap of writing pieces about the life that was lived, when their business is to discuss how the life was told." Recently there has been some attempt to discuss biography that way. But generally Edel's observation is a sad and perplexing fact. As Paul Mariani has noted, the absence of biographic criticism is a difficult phenomenon to explain in an age that takes pride in its allegiance to the critical act.

Part of the problem is that biography has fallen victim to the scourge of our age—overspecialization. Scanning the biographical landscape, we see professional historians pursuing lives in their chronological or thematic specialties, journalists and political scientists producing biographies in their areas of expertise and critics and English professors turning out studies of literary figures. We find scientists writing about scientists, philosophers about philosophers, theologians about theologians, music critics about rock-and-roll stars, and members of minorities about members of minorities ("How can *you* write about an Afro-American?" I have been asked more than once). Too often such specialists use a life mainly to advance an interpretation of an era, of a group or a movement, of a school or a body of literature. I think of what Ronnie Dugger's editor at Norton said about Dugger's projected multivolume life of Lyndon Johnson. "This isn't just biography," the editor informed *Publishers Weekly*. "It's an attempt to explain American and world history." Worse still, specialists who attempt biography too often write with cheerful disregard of the art of narration and a pronounced ignorance of the nature of the craft. To compound the problem, those who review biographies are all too frequently specialists themselves: they know the fields into which the subjects fall (the Civil War, race relations, Victorian literature) but little or nothing about the art of biography.

Still, as Vandiver observes, America has produced a

number of professional life-writers who have striven to master the craft, to bring their subjects alive with empathy and an artist's insight and sense of story, and who have produced significant bodies of work. By and large, though, Americans do not view such writers as practitioners of a noble literary genre that deserves the respect and attention given to fiction and poetry. We enjoy reading about lives, yes, but we do not pay enough attention to the manner of their telling, the skill and vision of their creators, and their place in the domain of literature. It is symptomatic of our time that a critic for the *New York Times Book Review* recently dismissed Lytton Strachey—the father of modern biography—as a minor and quite forgettable literary figure.

What we truly need, as Justin Kaplan said, is a new definition of literary biography, to include those lives that possess the literary merits Vandiver describes, biographies that attempt to simulate a human life through the magic of language, through character development and the depiction of interpersonal relationships, through graphic scenes, the telling quotation, the revealing detail, the power of suggestion, and dramatic narrative sweep; biographies that illuminate universal truths about humankind through the sufferings and triumphs of a single human being. Yes, we very much need to distinguish this kind of life-writing from analytical studies produced by specialists in other disciplines.

Should Americans develop a new tradition of literary or true biography, perhaps scholars in the academies will one day offer standard courses in the modern American biography. Perhaps critics of life-writing will study the narrative voice, the symbolism, the plot structure, the conception of character, the literary devices, the development and symmetry of Kaplan's Mark Twain and Walt Whitman, of Marquis James's Sam Houston and Andrew Jackson, of Mari Sandoz's Old Jules and Crazy Horse, of Frank Vandiver's Stonewall Jackson and Black Jack Pershing, of Nancy Mitford's Zelda and Jean Strouse's Alice James. The critic will remind us that these are the *biographers'* lives —*Kaplan's* Whitman, *Sandoz's* Crazy Horse, *Vandiver's* Pershing—and that the notion of "the definitive biography" is absurd. For the nature of life-writing—the process of one human being resurrecting another on the basis of human records, memories, and dreams—precludes a fixed and final portrait of any figure.

Which brings me to the special relationship between biographer and subject, that unique interaction of two humanities that Vandiver vividly described—and that our future critic of biography will explore in depth. Here I want to speak from my own experience, because the act of re-creating John Brown, Nat Turner, Abraham Lincoln, and Martin Luther King, Jr., profoundly changed my life. First, John Brown, made me understand how a man of intense Calvinist faith could hate a hateful thing like slavery, how he could become enraged at his country—a country based on the inalienable rights of man—for institutionalizing such a monstrous wrong. I am not a violent man, but in viewing Brown's embattled world through his eyes, sensing it through his hurts and furies, hearing the words of the Old Testament prophets that roared in his ears, I could appreciate why he would try to destroy slavery with the sword. In telling his story, I saw and felt the terrible cost of moral hypocrisy and retributive violence—of the tragic consequences of man's inhumanity to his fellow man.

Nat Turner, on the other hand, gave me melancholy insight into what it was like to be a slave, to be a victim of the very evil that so infuriated Brown. I felt Nat's sorrow and frustration as though they were my own. I anguished over his condition and that of his people and longed for his freedom all the more because I realized that he could never have it. As I described the prison of his life, I had the recurring image of a powerful angel with his wings nailed to the ground. At last, too frustrated and intelligent to remain somebody's property, aroused to a biblical fury by his own religious fantasies and the emotional revivalism of the time, Nat exploded at the system that oppressed him, inciting the most violent insurrection in southern history. With all his strength and human frailty, his liberating visions and bloody doom, Nat Turner lived a life that illustrated with blazing clarity what

Frederick Douglass said of slavery—that it brutalized everybody, black and white alike.

In contrast to Brown and Turner, Abraham Lincoln abhorred violence and worked all his life inside the American system, a system he deeply cherished because it allowed men like him the right to rise, to better their station in life and harvest the fruits of their toil. Yet Lincoln found himself trapped in a terrible dilemma. He personally hated slavery as much as Brown did and yet revered a political system that protected that very institution. He vacillated about when and how to resolve that dilemma, but after 1854 he never let his countrymen forget that slavery was a momentous *moral* problem that besmirched America's example before the world— and the bar of history. In the end he rooted out slavery with the most revolutionary measure ever to come from an American president.

I identified powerfully with the Lincoln of my story, for behind the myths, behind the god of marble and stone, I had discovered a man of rich humanity—a moral man who understood the complexities of human nature, a self-made man who was proud of his achievements, substantially wealthy, morbidly fascinated with madness, obsessed with death, troubled with bouts of melancholia, and gifted with a superb sense of history and a large talent for literary expression. I became so immersed in his life that I got depressed when he did; I hurt when he hurt. When I left my study after a day's writing in his world, with brass bands playing Civil War music in my head, I was stunned to find myself in the twentieth century.

For me, Lincoln's life seemed an endless battle against inner and outer adversity; it demonstrated that even those who rise to supreme heights have personal conflicts—identity crises, ambivalences, torments, setbacks, and even loss of will—which they have to agonize over and work their way through. In pensive moments I still think back over his life, back over those tornado years of civil war, and I can still see him standing as he often did at the White House windows, a haunted, harried man who did not know whether the conflict would ever end. Yet he fought it through to a total Union triumph, a triumph for popular government and a larger concept of the inalienable rights of man.

If anything, I identified even more with King, another impassioned man caught up in the problem of slavery and racial oppression and the struggle to right the country with its own ideals. Though he was as angry about racial oppression as Brown and Turner, King learned from Gandhi to channel his rage into a constructive and creative force. Armed with the strength to love, he set out to break the chain of hatred in the world that only produced more hatred in an endless spiral. If the chain could be broken, he contended, then a new day could begin when all of God's children would live together in a symphony of brotherhood. By word and deed he aroused the black masses and stirred the American conscience more than any other leader in his generation. More than anyone else, he helped make Lincoln's Emancipation Proclamation a political and social fact.

Like Lincoln, King had an epochal sense of history and a world view of striking insight. He repeatedly stressed the need to understand that all life is interconnected, that all people are tied together in a single garment of destiny, and that "we aren't going to have peace on earth until we recognize this basic fact of the interrelated structure of reality." Finally, he set an example of extraordinary courage—the courage to confront evil in oneself as well.

King's teachings affected me personally, for I suffered a devastating tragedy in my life while I was writing his, and I almost succumbed to a paralyzing bitterness. But I learned from his example how to love again and "keep on keepin' on" despite my shattered dreams. In a strange and miraculous way the very man I re-created became a warm, sympathetic friend.

I came to know King so intimately that I spoke to him in my dreams. I even fell into his speech rhythms when I talked about him in interviews and on the lecture circuit. And when he died in my story, I was stricken with an overwhelming sense of loss, as though a member of my family had been killed. After I sent him home to Atlanta, to be buried near his Grandmother Williams, whom he had loved so as a boy, I left my typewriter and staggered into my living room filled with grief, unable to believe or to bear what had happened. And I cried.

For me, biography has been not only high literary and historical adventure but deep personal experience as well. In the sixteen years it has taken me to fashion my quartet of lives, I have come to believe—as Yeats suggested—that "nothing exists but a stream of souls, that all knowledge is biography."

JEAN STROUSE

Frank Vandiver has observed that modern biography seems "mired in motivation" and that efforts to graft psychological and social sciences onto biography amount to a warping of the art. I agree with both those observations and find most attempts at "psychohistory" and "psychobiography" hopelessly reductionistic, jargon-ridden, and heavy-handed. However, questions of motivation do raise their querulous heads these days, in ways they did not in nineteenth-century biography—precisely because we now have more useful ways of looking at and thinking about what makes people tick than nineteenth-century biographers had. The question of psychological motivation in biography is useful not as *explanation* but as a way of opening up the human dimensions of the past. I would not agree with Durkheim's statement, alluded to by Mr. Vandiver, that history can elucidate psychology but never the reverse: the problem lies not with psychology itself but with the artfulness (or, more commonly, the lack of artfulness) in a writer's *use* of psychological or psychoanalytic insight.

Mr. Vandiver asks why biography is so popular just now. One answer may be that biography has taken the place the novel used to fill. Nineteenth-century novels—by George Eliot, Henry James, William Dean Howells, Herman Melville, George Meredith—provided readers with large slices of life in which questions of character, motivation, morality, social pressure, and internal conflict could be explored in great depth. People read, and still read, those books for the pleasure of imagining their way into other lives, other times, other locations—and for what comes back into their own lives from those journeys. Most modern novels—all bare bones and spare parts—do not provide that kind of satisfaction. Modern biographies often do.

The question of motivation, in biography as in fiction, must be handled with artful delicacy, if it is to elucidate history and private life—but, one way or another, I think that it does need to be handled, for it has everything to do with character, as Mr. Vandiver has been discussing character: with what made this particular person respond to his time, his family, his social, economic, and personal surroundings in just the ways that are worth thinking about long after he lived. Looking into the internal dynamics of character need not mean guessing or pretending to know what somebody felt or thought at any given point: assessments about personal dynamics need not necessarily even enter the text of the biography. If the author deeply understands his subject, however, in the empathic way Mr. Vandiver has recommended, his own questions about why X happened rather than Y and about how specific life choices were arrived at should inform his assembling of the material in such a way that the character of his subject will come into full view with the vividness of fiction. Without this complex understanding biographical portraits lack dimension—becoming mere records of "this happened and then that happened," without a unifying sense of personality.

From the interviews with the other participants in this institute published in the *Texas Humanist*, I gather that we are all in agreement about how real and almost palpable the subject becomes in the biographer's imagination. *Alice James* was my first biography, and I was surprised to find, about a year or two into my work, what powerful and sometimes problematic presences she and the other members of her family had assumed in my life. I eventually came to think that if I could not see and hear one of them in my mind I had not somehow "got" him or her yet. They even insinuated themselves into my dreams, and the ghost of Henry, Jr., kept peering over my shoulder—sometimes simply hovering there, as if to keep me honest. Although he made me more than a little nervous, he presented no insuperable problems—but Alice's troublesome personality did.

She was not an obvious subject for a biography. She did nothing to inspire admiration, she left no great work, and she did not lead an exemplary life in any sense of the term—

she herself concluded that her life had been a failure. Nonetheless, she interested me—as a character, a spirit, a member
of that extraordinary family, a psychological puzzle, and a
sentient individual who expressed in various forms very real
responses to the changing shapes of nineteenth-century
American society. Not surprisingly, she was extremely difficult to live with, both for her contemporaries and for me,
virtually "living" with her long after her death. She made a
career of invalidism, forcing the people she cared about to
take care of her, claiming exemption for the ordinary requirements of coping with life. In my own life I do not have
much patience with people who behave that way, and when I
first ran into trouble with Alice, the biographer Justin Kaplan,
who was living near me in Cambridge, said, "Just remember,
you can kill her off whenever you like." That was an extremely useful thing to hear, but still at a certain point in the
writing of the book I came to a dead stop. After a few weeks
I began to see that I wanted Alice's life to turn out somehow
better than it had. She possessed a fine mind, a great deal of
energy, a passionate interest in history, and strongly compet-
itive instincts. Why, I found myself demanding of both myself and her, couldn't she just pull up her socks and get on
with something, instead of wasting her life being sick with
vague prostrations, headaches, and violent nervous break-
downs? That question was a real response to Alice, and it is
probably the one I would have had if I had actually met her.
However, it did not lead me toward any greater understanding of or sympathy with the way her life did in fact turn out—
at first. Eventually, however, I came to see that I was not just
entertaining an irrelevant desire for a happy ending. Alice
herself—not to get too metaphysical about this—had done
something to me, and I had a great deal to learn from my
response. As you relive a life, reimagining it step by step, you
have, I think, to perceive all the paths not taken in order to
understand the paths that were taken, and that was part of
my difficulty. But also the measure of Alice's ambition, in that
family, to achieve something of her own, to be somehow more
than an invalid, a girl, a waste—all that was a measure of her

bitter sense of failure; and although it was in coming to terms with that sense of failure that she achieved her real stature and interest as a character, it was also true that she desperately wanted some more conventional measure of success for her life. She herself wanted it to come out somehow *better*. In order fully to perceive Alice James on her own terms and in her own contexts, I had to experience those conflicts for myself. She was not simply a victim of her time or sex: other women in the mid-nineteenth century managed to write novels, become doctors, raise happy families, find some sense of satisfaction. Understanding just why Alice James was not able to do any of those things was crucial to seeing her life as a whole. And her life turned out to reveal a great deal about the entire James family, about the post–Civil War era in New England, about women's history, and about nervous disorders and medical thinking in the late nineteenth century. But I think all the biographers at this institute would agree that without the prism of individual character through which to perceive them all those secondary themes would seem like empty abstractions.

Alice James's life required a particularly psychological approach—more so, it turned out, than I had anticipated at the start—because the story of her life (like many of the stories in her brother's novels) is one in which nothing really happens except changes in perception and consciousness. To deal adequately with that kind of story, I found the insights of psychoanalysis extremely helpful as "deep background," though I was careful not to use analytic jargon in the text itself (I was pleased to find that a reviewer in the *Times Literary Supplement* scolded me for not being Freudian enough). However, although I found psychoanalytic theory useful, I also mined social history, literature, medicine, and a number of other fields for all they were worth, and I would not want to make a prescription of any of them. Clearly, other kinds of lives raise other kinds of questions. I would, however, stick by the proposition that fully to understand *character*, which Frank Vandiver has called the "luminous hallmark of soldiers" (and, I might add, of neurasthenic invalids), it is essential to look beneath the surface of daily life. "To live other people's lives is nothing," wrote Henry James, "unless we live over their perceptions, live over the growth, the change, the varying intensity of the same—since it was *by* these things they themselves lived."

The Humanities, the Professions, and the Uses of Biography

Steven Weiland

Lives lived whole are the most satisfying but also, according to William Butler Yeats, the most difficult to achieve. He presents in "The Choice" (1933) the private and professional interests which divide us:

> The Intellect of man is forced to choose
> Perfection of the life, or of the work,
> And if it take the second must refuse
> A heavenly mansion, raging in the dark.
> When all that story's finished, what's the news?
> In luck or out the toil has left its mark
> That old perplexity an empty purse,
> Or the day's vanity, the night's remorse.

Even if we are more sanguine than Yeats about the results of devotion to a career—if we are less vain and remorseful than he proposes—we can recognize in this poem that, just as our work will reveal its distinctive "mark," so will the benefits be limited by strict devotion to it.

Humanists and Professionals

Choosing perfection as a humanist is no less difficult. For "humanities" and "professions" are words with great traditions but cloudy meanings. Much of the confusion about both derives from our current habit of talking about them as if each were an integrated, unified whole. They are not. The humanities are a collection of disciplines—history, philosophy, literary criticism, and others—sometimes closely related, sometimes not—whose methods, intentions, and practitioners vary as much as the many kinds of work—medical, legal, religious, military, scientific, and others—that we group under the heading "professions." Practitioners—humanists or professionals—can be contemplative or active, engaged or detached, ethical or unscrupulous, sophisticated or superficial, capacious or parochial. To appreciate what a humanist or professional does, we need first to know his or her subject and the methods that shape it.

It makes little sense to speak of humanists apart from the particular disciplines that they practice, and it was for this reason that William Schaeffer, past executive secretary of the Modern Language Association, recently declined to be identified as one. He declared his distaste for the rhetorical excesses of some supporters of the humanities. "What I fear," Schaeffer says, "is that all this carrying on about humanistic perspectives and humanistic values, far from enhancing our professional concerns, tends to make mush out of clearly defined disciplines." In other words, a humanist is by definition usually professional, but a professional is not necessarily a humanist. According to this strict-constructionist approach, we would do well to abandon the term "humanist" and all that it suggests about a privileged sense of "values" and "perspectives" and to stress instead the interests and activities of the particular disciplines. Schaeffer's advice to humanists is to "talk less about what we are, which isn't all that much, and begin to stress what we do."

Most professionals, of course, prefer to be identified by their profession—we would not indiscriminately seek a "professional" opinion from an engineer or agricultural economist on a public issue outside his or her field the way we sometimes do of a teacher or scholar in the humanities who is assumed by some to possess particular virtues ("values" and "perspective") simply because he or she is a humanist. Professionalism is first of all particular, but in the last few decades there has been increased attention to some generic features, for instance, the ways in which the major professions reflect social, political, and economic ideologies, maintain solidarity and control over their domains, and establish patterns of socialization through their training programs. Although it may be said that the interest of humanists in the professions reflects some public distrust of them, professionals still carry unique and widely respected responsibilities precisely because they are assumed to see the world differently from the way others see it. As Everett Hughes, the influential scholar of the professions, says, "The professional is expected to think objectively and inquiringly about matters which may be, for the layman, subject to orthodoxy and sentiment."

Opening a case with an argument about definitions can stall it in quibbling. What difference does it make, after all, who is a humanist or who is a professional? Yet needless imprecision about the uses of the disciplines of the humanities has contributed to misleading expectations about what they are and do and has also given an opening to frightened fundamentalists looking for "secular humanists" under every bed. We should also care about the meaning and implications of the professions and professionalism because professionals affect our lives and because the right to a professional identity has been a matter of great personal and social importance in America. Henry James, Sr., was a philosopher and scholar, but he apparently did not impress Henry James, Jr., who envied schoolmates whose fathers had conventional careers. To his son's inquiries about his work Henry, Sr., would respond with amusement: "Say I'm a philosopher, say I'm a seeker for truth, say I'm a lover of my kind, say I'm an author of books if you like; or, best of all, just say I'm a Student." Henry, Jr., found this answer "abject" because an easily understood job or profession supplies domestic, as well as individual and social identities. Thinking about professions, therefore, requires more than a determination to be exact in defining them. Their origins, practices, and impact are what should concern us, and in these matters the humanities, through the interpretative work of teachers and scholars in individual disciplines, can help.

The Psychiatric Self

Among the many styles of interpretation (including the poetic) of the professions, I want here to cite just three: historical, operational, and biographical. From the first we get accounts of particular professions and sometimes attempts to synthesize historically their generic elements; from the second we get functional or operational analyses of current practices and training in the professions; from the third, which in some ways combines the best of the first two, we get vivid and particular accounts, often of the origins of a profession or a great innovation in it or of its ideals and standards as they are embodied in an exemplary practitioner.

Each deserves attention, but I wish to offer only two-thirds of an example, that is, two of the styles of interpretation applied to a single profession. My case from the professions is the profession of cases: psychiatry and, of course, psychoanalysis. Psychoanalysis is a relatively new profession, not even a century old, and psychiatry is perhaps a century older as a distinct medical specialty (if we except the activities of witch doctors and the custodial activities—for centuries in the West—of poorly trained professional physicians interested in the deranged). Freud himself termed psychoanalytic psychiatry one of the three "impossible professions," along with education and government. He wrote to Oskar Pfister, a Swiss pastor who became an early disciple: "I wish to protect analysis from the doctors and from the priests. I should like to hand it over to a profession which does not yet exist, a profession of lay curers of souls who need not be doctors and should not be priests." So some uncertainty about capacity and qualifications was built into psychoanalysis from its beginning, and as a profession it has continued to question itself, as the recent work of Robert Jay Lifton, Robert Coles, Allen Wheelis, and others demonstrates.

Histories of professions tend to strive for inclusiveness and balance, often in century-by-century, decade-by-decade accounts of the development of specialized techniques, institutions, training methods, innovative leaders, and a skeptical but finally receptive public. In psychiatry its leaders struggled both for public acceptance and for a place within the medical profession. It is the latter that the distinguished analyst Franz

Alexander had in mind in this statement in his *History of Psychiatry* (1966):

As the momentum of awareness and involvement gathers, it becomes increasingly evident not only that psychiatry has come of age but also that our civilization may have entered an age of psychiatry. This evolution has meant more than the betterment of psychiatry; it has meant the advancement of all medicine. Man, the benefactor, has come a long way from the first crude probings of the prehistoric witch doctors and ancient physician-priests.

His subject, Alexander says, is the "saga" of psychiatry. Yet the predictable rhythm and outcome of such an approach allow little room for the consideration of issues and presentation of conflicts of interest to truly inquisitive outsiders.

The natural complement to the historical approach is the approach that focuses on current professional practice. We can admire the results as scholars and be grateful for them as consumers. A good example is *Becoming Psychiatrists: The Professional Transformation of Self* (1980), in which sociologist Donald Light states that training for the psychiatric profession is "unusual in the degree to which one's whole personality, style, personal history, and future outlook are subject to intense scrutiny and recasting. This differs significantly from engineering school or from learning to be a meat packer. . . . Some callings are a way of life; others merely get a job done."

Light's study ably blends his thorough knowledge of the large and impressive scholarship in psychiatric training with his findings from a year spent as a participant-observer in the psychiatric residency program of a large New England hosptial. Becoming a psychiatrist, Light discovered, amounts to becoming an unusually complicated kind of professional owing to the fundamental obscurity of the discipline in relation to its high ideals and public expectations. The psychiatrist, he acknowledges, should also fit the description of the model physician, according to which he or she is "compassionate, sympathetic, perceptive, and understanding, and likes

human beings . . . a person of culture." But Light also recognizes the vagueness of such a summary of professional and
human qualities (not to mention its lack of humility). It is the
nature of psychiatry's imperfections as a profession that interests him; for instance, the gap between the claims of
professional training and the actual requirements of the work
and its results. For the special aptitude needed, especially for
therapeutic and advanced theoretical work, is antecedent to
what can be conveyed in orthodox professional preparations.
"The psychiatrist as a person," Light says, "is more important
than the psychiatrist as a technician or scientist. What he *is*
has much more effect upon his patients than anything he
does." As in painting or fine carpentry, therefore, becoming
a psychiatrist is a process not so much of learning the necessary techniques as of fulfilling one's natural capacity or gift.

Like other critics of medicine, Light objects not to this
style of professional development but to the assumptions in
many aspects of professional training that stress the primacy
of technical proficiency and scientific rigor. Among the
professional models he describes, it is not surprising that he
prefers the "intellectual" psychiatrists to the "managerial" ones,
preferring those who are interested in all the implications of
their work to those who are fully satisfied by the therapeutic
progress they make with their patients. The intellectual psychiatrists are unlikely to need to have pointed out to them
what Light terms the great issues of psychiatric socialization:
"the tension between relating to the patient as a person or as
a case; the conflict between management and psychotherapy;
a primary focus on the curing process versus preoccupation
with therapeutic technique; and the tension between seeing
a case in terms of a patient's illness or in terms of one's own
neurosis." The resolution of these issues provides the structure of all psychiatric careers, but the process begins in
professional training and initial clinical experience.

It is hard to know what to think, then, of the residency
program that Light observed, which he describes as "basi-
cally holistic, diffuse, seductive, positive, and intense, making
for a deep, broad reshaping of professional identity." But while

he admires the comprehensive impact of the training, Light is nonetheless disheartened by the flaws in some of its products. Psychiatrists, patients, institutions, and public policies related to treatment of mental illness and to professional education often reflect the managerial style. Hence, from his perspective as a sociologist Light endorses this kind of question about psychiatric practice, one among many that psychiatrists should ask themselves: "Do I know the difference between where my knowledge is inadequate and where the field's knowledge is inadequate?" Such a question—even William Schaeffer would agree—represents the perspective gained from looking at one activity by using the methods of another. That will make Light a humanist in the eyes of some, but there is no sign in his work that general humanistic "values" have displaced the professional habits of intelligent and timely sociology.

Light's technique also allows the young professionals and their teachers to speak for themselves; hence his interpretations can be seen to emerge from the actual experience of professionalization. The careful balance of the concrete and the abstract is another sign that "perspective" is a product of scholarly or artistic techniques. "My fantasy," one young psychiatric resident says, "is that someday I'll have no feelings about the case." Another says of his decision to become a psychoanalyst, "You make a commitment of faith, like a monk." And one of their supervisors says to them ruefully, "The patient's biases are regarded as pathological, while yours are called 'knowledge.' It's hard to get together under those circumstances." Light resists cynicism because he knows that all professions have their extremes of technique and frequently capitalize on lay ignorance of the content of expertise. But one way he acknowledges the limits of psychiatric professionalism is by recommending that it incorporate some of the techniques of the humanities: "It is accurate to say that in most cases, psychiatrists learn to diagnose from anecdotal material, with little training in the rigors of psychological inference which historians or other professionals who work with case studies use." And while psychiatry (and psychoanalysis) could benefit from such a technique, as a profession it has also depended on another class of humanists—biographers—to shape public understanding of what it does. In this regard psychiatry is like all other professions that rely on extraordinary powers, on charismatic authority in the lay community. Because of their "weak technical paradigm" (Light's way of saying that the theory is unproven), psychiatry and psychoanalysis stress their heroic feats of expertise. The giants—like Freud—come to symbolize the profession.

Freud: Master and Model

The inevitable format for the making of such symbols is, of course, biography, the third style of humanistic interest in the professions. Without question this style has been the most influential in promoting professional ideals in and out of psychoanalysis. Soon after the publication in the mid-1950s of Ernest Jones's landmark biography of Freud, the literary critic Lionel Trilling expressed envy of Freud's followers. "To have [the psychoanalytic movement's] history in mind, made actual and dramatic in the person of Freud himself, must give members of the profession a lively belief in intellectual possibility, and in the personal nature of cultural achievement, a wondering happy awareness of what a person can do toward the renovation of a culture." Yet the purposes, emphasis, and tone of biographies of Freud are now themselves the subject of considerable scholarly debate. These methodological issues were made especially clear in 1980, when Ronald Clark published his comprehensive and conventional biography, whose very title, *Freud: The Man and the Cause*, suggests Clark's interest in fortifying the traditional interpretation of Freud as a determined pioneer inventing a profession as he gradually broke down public and medical resistance to his revolutionary theories. At the same time Frank Sulloway, a historian of science, published *Freud: Biologist of the Mind*, an iconoclastic biographical and critical study whose two major themes are, first, that Freud was actually a crypto-biologist whose theories depend more heavily on neuroanatomy and the Darwinian legacy than his modern interpretors acknowledge and, second, that Freud's biographers have often eschewed accurate scientific interpretation of his work in favor of making and perpetuating a variety of myths about his life: that he lived in professional isolation early in his career, that his self-analysis was an unprecedented and utterly herculean task, and that he broke with several disciples for legitimate intellectual reasons.

In his own way Sulloway supports the thesis that biography is a form of compensation to professions burdened with weak theory. In his view Freudian biography is an "interlocking web of legend: the myths of the hero and of Freud as pure psychologist are the heart of the epistemological politics that have pervaded the entire psychoanalytic revolution." While he does not quite charge Freud's biographers with falsifying the record, Sulloway's conspiracy theory does suggest that biography can be distorted by professional interests. In other words, the biographers of innovative thinkers and professionals face ethical questions as integral to the humanities as the scholarly tools they employ.

Perhaps Freud himself foresaw problems of this kind when he wrote in 1935 to an aspiring biographer, Arnold Zweig:

I am alarmed by the threat that you want to become my biographer—you who have so much better and more important things to do, you, who can establish monarchs and who can survey the brutal folly of mankind from a lofty vantage point; no, I am far too fond of you to permit such a thing. Anyone who writes a biography is committed to lies, concealments, hypocrisy, flattery, and even to hiding his own lack of understanding, for biographical truth does not exist, and if it did we could not use it. Truth is unobtainable, mankind does not deserve it, and in any case is not our Prince Hamlet right when he asks who would escape whipping were he used after his desert.

This letter is frequently quoted but usually without the unintended irony of the remark about establishing monarchs. Indeed, a psychological interpretation might propose that we ignore Freud's false modesty and suggest that he feared that biography might not always conform to his own understanding of his role in the psychoanalytic movement. Zweig's response has also escaped attention. Naturally he agreed with his hero, but he notes that another reason for not writing the biography was Freud's own plan to include in a supplement to his brief *Autobiographical Study* (1925) an account of what Zweig apparently thought to be the central biographical issue: Freud's relations with disciples who differed with him on crucial points of psychoanalytic theory. This narrow idea of biographical intent suggests why biographies need to be written again and again, why some distance in time and some detachment in point of view together with empathy are indispensable to them.

There is yet a second irony in Freud's resistance to biography. The profession that he invented supplied an important tool to biographers (who often rightly warn about its simply mechanical use), yet he resisted its application to his life in any hands but his own. Freud was himself a biographer, though his famous case studies and brief portraits of Leonardo da Vinci and Moses might properly be called character studies. In his *Autobiographical Study* he made this assessment of the uses and limits of what is now called psychobiography: "What psychoanalysis was able to do was to take the interrelations between the impressions of the artist's life, his chance experiences, and his work, and from them construct his constitution and the impulses at work in it—that is to say, that part of him which he shared with all men." Yet he cautioned that "the layman may perhaps expect too much from analysis in this respect, for it must be admitted that it throws no light upon the two problems which probably interest him the most. It can do nothing towards elucidating the nature of the artistic gift, nor can it explain the means by which the artist works—artistic technique." Similarly, Hanns Sachs, one of Freud's loyal disciples, a lawyer and psychoanalyst whose biography of Freud is subtitled *Master and Friend*, states candidly that he has no idea what exactly in Freud's life supplied his professional motivations.

Yet for Freud it is the work that counts. He claimed that

the real meaning of his *Autobiographical Study* was that it showed "how psychoanalysis came to be the whole content of my life" and that "no personal experiences of mine are of interest in comparison to my relations with that science." Careers dominate most biographies, though Jean Strouse has recently demonstrated in *Alice James* how to make a life without a profession vivid and historically important. One of the great virtues of Ronald Steel's *Walter Lippmann and the American Century*, another recent biography, is its presentation of an important kind of journalistic career, a tool for understanding not only Lippmann but also others who do his kind of work, though usually not nearly as well. Steel's book defines a profession in nearly its ideal form, and in light of historical circumstances, the important themes of public life, and the peculiar talents and interests of Lippmann himself. In other words, it demonstrates what the humanities, through biography, bring to the professions.

No study of the history of a profession can illuminate the origins and operation of professional ideals as well as the cumulative or contrasting effects of well-written individual lives. Consider what we can learn about the competing ideals and professional demands of physics as a profession from the study of biographies of Einstein and Oppenheimer, in law of Louis D. Brandeis and William O. Douglas, in religion of Ghandi and Thomas Merton, in psychiatry of Freud and Harry Stack Sullivan. Indeed, Sullivan is the subject of a new and authoritative biography, *Psychiatrist of America*, by his colleague and protégé Helen Swick Perry. Like Freud, Sullivan was skeptical about the capacity of biography to provide accurate portraits. In 1947, less than two years before he died, he said that "biography usually fails to integrate its subject person with the significant others who facilitated and handicapped his durable achievements as a contributor to culture history, and rarely indicates whence came his skills and limitations in the interpersonal relations which made his contribution effective." Sullivan insists that only attention to the "culture complex" will give biography social or psychological meaning. The study of Freud and the advancement of psychoanalysis in the 1940s did not, according to Sullivan, reflect such high standards. "The phenomenon of Freud," he said, "without its setting in the contemporary society of Vienna has been followed by the phenomena of Freud's evangelists and Freud's detractors, also without sensitivity to the nuances of cultural differences within the major context of the Western World."

Perry's fidelity to Sullivan's views (and generous attitude toward his frequently awkward prose) are evident throughout her biography. She describes in illuminating detail his small-town New York State background and its influence on his choice of a career and professional goals. Sullivan's multiple and complex relations with colleagues in and out of his field (one said that Sullivan was a social scientist whose specialty was psychiatry) are set against the enduring elements of his background. The rural culture from which Sullivan came contrasted sharply with the urbane, Europe-influenced scientific culture in which he worked. In the design of her biography Perry suggests the applicability to individual lives within one society of Sullivan's guide to intercultural analysis:

Individual differences, especially those which are principally matters of language and customs in people from widely separate parts of the world, may be extremely impressive and may present [a] great handicap to discovering the significant differences in relative adequacy and appropriateness of action in interpersonal relations, which constitute extraordinary success, average living, or mental disorder.

While she depends on the theory of interpersonal relations for which Sullivan is now best known, Perry recognizes the difficulties of reaching what Sullivan himself called the "immutably private" that can never be completely captured even by psychological biography.

Sullivan's career matured between 1920 and 1940, the period during which Freudian psychoanalysis was integrated into American psychiatry. At the same time many European analysts—some fleeing the Nazis—emigrated to the United States. Internecine struggles over theory and competition with their new American colleagues were not uncommon. Perry endorses the idea that Freud's autocratic behavior as founder of psychoanalysis and guardian of its basic principles was to blame for the schisms. In contrast, Sullivan's democratic and benign temperament meant that his influence over professional colleagues was limited. Some of those with whom he worked closely—Erich Fromm and Karen Horney, for example—were ostracized by other analysts as apostates. Perry claims that "political feelings were so strong that many clinicians who make generous use of Sullivan's theories are still loathe to ascribe their insights to him." The problems she faced as Sullivan's first biographer, in light of the traditions of the study of Freud and other psychiatrists and psychoanalysts, are evident in her admission that "many of Sullivan's colleagues thought of him as being one or another of these three kinds of characters: a withdrawn and cantankerous drunk; a somewhat pretentious high-stepper and sophisticate; the kindest, most considerate man who ever lived."

In her portrait Sullivan is frequently lonely and despairing, struggling to overcome his obscure social background, marginal professional education, and ambivalence about orthodox Freudian technique. That he succeeded at all, Perry suggests, is testimony to his native intelligence and tenacity and the peculiar circumstances of American culture. Sullivan's career illustrates for her, therefore, an important principle: The "need for success is not a simple materialistic grind, as it is often portrayed, but the pressure and the desire to prove, in this diversified, democratic society, that one's own forbears are as good as anybody else's; that regardless of his country of origin—either recent or remote—each person has the right and the capacity to be successful." Sullivan's theoretical and clinical achievements, while substantial, do not approach Freud's. Yet, as Perry's biography demonstrates, his life nonetheless displays important private and public themes in the development of modern psychiatry.

Conclusion: The Double Law

Like Helen Perry, Freud's biographers have generally resisted the temptation to write psychoanalytic biographies of their subject. This apparent paradox is explainable simply in terms of the requirements of judicious scholarship. Critics of psychoanalytic biography often note its tendency to reductiveness, the misguided application of quasiscientific formulas to idiosyncratic lives. Yet the best psychoanalytic biographies, like those by Erik H. Erikson, never sacrifice historical and political events to family and psychological dynamics or to themes of individual development. In seeking the common ground between clinical and historical interests, the biographer must learn to see his or her subject's achievements and crises as, in Erikson's terms, "communal events characteristic of a given historical period." The history of a profession is a timely biographical theme, but not, of course, one synthetic enough to carry by itself a full life history.

For poet Howard Nemerov, like Yeats, professionalism is problematic, and to contemplate mastery is to know its limits. Its permanence and desire for detachment are conveyed in the questions that open Nemerov's poem "The Master at a Mediterranean Port":

> What . . . constitutes mastery?
> The perdurable fire of a style?
> A rock that the incessant sea
> Thunders against for fifteen hundred years?
> Or maybe, manners that can speak
> Of excrement without offense.

Yet, observing the water washing up on the boats, docks, and shoreline, Nemerov proposes the open sea and the harbor as a double image of mastery, of its conflicting but complementary meanings, applicable to all kinds of knowing and doing. The open sea

> . . . is a disputed field, it changes sides,
> Is turbulent, is unreflecting, deep
> And deep and deep, and boils at interruption
> Of wind or keel.

In the apostrophe that follows are combined recognition of the power of professions, their limits, even their tendency to mislead or to obscure reality.

O valuable glass,
Clear harbor, floor not altogether false:
Respect the doubleness of these laws.
Mastery, the master, his image and his stance,
His way of seeing, his eloquent speech:
. . . these are no perdurable fire,
No steadfast rock. They are
The manners of a time, an age perhaps
Ready to die, a classical notation
For the harbor glass, the law against the truth.

Do not be taken completely, Nemerov says, with the expertness of experts (the professionalism of professionals), for they sometimes block the truth, but, on the other hand, do not ignore the truth they bring, which may not be permanent but is usually pertinent.

As styles of thought and action, the humanities are deep and turbulent (like the open sea) and as clear and exactingly or artfully shaped as glass. They are at the same time a danger and a shelter. Our professionalism, whatever our particular fields, lies in taking the temptation of the deep water while we improve the moorings—especially the scholarly and biographical ones—of the harbor.

Biography: The Self and the Sacred Canopy

JAMES F. VENINGA

"At its best," says Frank Vandiver, "biography brings a touch of humanity from the past and can, if deftly done, offer a glimpse of humanity in microcosm." Unlike its distant cousins—profiles of living politicians, Hollywood stars, and other notables, books that tend to stimulate prurient instincts—a good biography can lead to a more thoughtful understanding of human life. The avid reader of true biography evidences a curiosity about the nature and meaning of human life as well as a special interest in particular lives. What we learn through biography, and how we learn, needs examining.

In my reading of recounted lives, certain patterns have emerged about the kinds of insight into human life that are gained through biography. I shall discuss three such patterns, though the reader may detect others as well.

I shall deny the temptation to discuss the obvious significance of biography for the scholar: that of a deepened understanding of one's academic field. If one teaches nineteenth-century American social history, Robert Abzug's biography of Theodore Weld surely enhances that person's scholarly pursuits. If one's academic interest is in modern military history, Frank Vandiver's biography of Black Jack Pershing makes an invaluable contribution. Although many interesting questions arise about the relationship between biography and academic fields, I shall confine myself to the implications of biography for more general humanistic inquiry. I have in mind the lay reader, regardless of profession, occupation, or intellectual interests. For the person whose life includes humanistic inquiry, the central question is, What is gained through the reading of biography?

Patterns of Insight

Biography provides us with insight into how other people have given shape to their lives; our knowledge of human personality is deepened. Hagiographic and moralistic biography provides little such insight, for we are given a false portrait of the subject, one that lacks truth and objectivity. The personality is camouflaged by the writer's motives. A biography that is a mere chronicle of a person's life also fails in this regard; we learn many facts about the subject's life—presented in "proper" sequence—but the real person of flesh, bone, and spirit is missing.

Thoughtful, carefully crafted biography seeks, as Jean Strouse says, "to illuminate aspects of a life from inside." The biographer's insight into the psychology of the subject is requisite to providing the reader with an understanding of how that person managed the vicissitudes of life and shaped his or her life amidst the numerous realities that impinged upon that life.

Leon Edel argues that in every life there is a manifest myth and a secret, inner myth. It is the task of the biographer to move behind the manifest myth—the façade—to bring forth the inner myth, the inner life. This is an extraordinarily difficult challenge, demanding great insight and skill, especially since biographers are frequently confronted by "the oppressive weight" of archival material and by lives that sought to hide the inner myth and to extol the manifest myth. Faced with these problems, the biographer must ask the right questions, and his method, as Edel says, "is related to the methods of Sherlock Holmes and also to those of Sigmund Freud." For Edel,

Biography stated in these terms begins to become more than a recital of facts, more than a description of an individual's minute doings, more than a study of achievement, when we allow ourselves to glimpse the myths within and behind the individual, the inner myth we all create in order to live, the myth that tells us we have some being, some selfhood, some goal, something to strive for beyond the fulfillments of food or sex or creature comforts.

Justin Kaplan likewise argues for the necessity of discovering the inner life, the "naked self." Kaplan takes his clue from Yeats: "There is some one myth for every man, which, if we but knew it, would make us understand all that he did and thought." To unravel that myth (or myths) is to find the key to the story of a life. The good biographer, argues Kaplan, must go to the "underpinnings of personal mythologies," to the supporting structures of beliefs and values.

Biographies that evoke full lives—inner and outer persons—provide us with knowledge about how other persons have shaped their existence. We see the process by which that shape comes into being. We may like that shape, be disgusted by it, or stand in total awe of it, but, in an immediate sense, our reaction to the shape of the life is of less importance than the fact that we *see* the shape and the process that led to it.

This knowledge is unique, and it can be argued that only through biography do we have the opportunity to see a human life in its totality, a human life in its final shape, a life lived on the basis of inner myths. It is impossible to gain such knowledge of oneself and nearly impossible in regard to one's family members, friends, or associates, even if these persons no longer live. We may, in the case of a deceased parent, for instance, have a firm grasp of the course of his or her life and the dynamics of the personality, if our insight and psychological skills of analysis are up to the task, but rarely do we have access to the kind of evidence that skilled writers use in developing a biography or spend the time and attain the objectivity needed to understand fully how the life of that parent was shaped.

It is remarkable that this knowledge of another life may come to us in a weekend of reading. The biographer may spend five, ten, or fifteen years studying, analyzing, and writing; the reader devours the results of this scholarly effort over a few days' time. We may spend an adult lifetime thinking now and then about our grandfather's life, piecing together history and personality; we come to know Abraham Lincoln, Walt Whitman, or Theodore Weld in a matter of hours in ways that we can never know our grandfather.

And what are the specifics of this knowledge? To use Edel's distinction, we learn much more than the events and acts that express the outer myth. We learn more than a life history. We glimpse inside the person to see a life unfold. We see the influence of environment on personality and of personality on environment. We discover anew the nature and meaning of the seasons of life. We see the fragility of the human psyche as it braces against the strong winds that would blow it asunder. We see the joy of success and the tribulation of failure. We see the magic of love and the power of hate.

We see individuals in pursuit of wholeness and meaning, and we trace their steps along this journey. We see individuals devoid of purpose, and we follow them to their fateful end. If the subject is magnanimous and mature, we learn why. If the subject is cruel and deranged, we learn the reason. If the subject is pursued by demons, we have an explanation, if not a reason. If the subject glides through life as easily as one could ever hope, we find a clue, if not a cause.

This knowledge, of course, comes to us by way of art, not science. The reasons, the explanations, the causes are ultimately those of the artist, not the scientist. Insight gained from biography derives from the artist's vision of a life lived on the basis of inner myths. The more we know of the subject's soul, the greater the writer's gift. The more we know of how the subject sought to shape his or her life, the greater the writer's vision.

Good biography provides us with insight of another age. Frank Vandiver notes that biography is "history made personal," and to support his thesis concerning the use of biography in elucidating history, he refers to Barbara W. Tuchman's essay "Biography as a Prism of History."

Tuchman's interest in biography lies in its ability to serve as a "vehicle for exhibiting an age." Biography "attracts and holds the reader's interest in the larger subject." Tuchman clarifies this point by referring to her own biographical studies. In *A Distant Mirror*, Enguerrand de Coucy VII, the re-

markable fourteenth-century French Knight, "supplies leads
to every subject—marriage and divorce, religion, insurrection, literature, Italy, England, war, politics, and a wonderful
range of the most interesting people of his time, from pope
to peasant." In *The Proud Tower*, House Speaker Thomas B.
Reed provides the means to understand fundamental ideas
that helped shape America: "Reed led, through the anti-
imperialist cause, to Samuel Gompers, E. L. Godkin, Charles
Eliot Norton, William James, Charles William Eliot, . . . Carl
Schurz, Andrew Carnegie, Moorfield Storey, and to their attitudes and beliefs about America." Thus biography is a most
useful tool in understanding history and clarifying forces,
ideas, and values that expressed an age, a country, a civilization.

Unfortunately, Tuchman's thesis that biography serves
as a "prism of history" leads her to depreciate biography as
psychological study. Tuchman claims that Lytton Strachey's
"influence on psychological interpretation . . . has been followed to excess." She argues that "since Strachey, and of course
Freud, the hidden secrets, especially if they are shady, are the
biographer's goal and the reader's delight." She pokes fun at
Erik H. Erikson's biographical work: "A whole book is written to show that Martin Luther was constipated. This may be
fascinating to some, but is it, in fact, historically significant?"

Here we find the sharpest contrast between those who
argue that the primary knowledge gained through biography is an understanding of how other persons have shaped
their lives amidst the realities of human existence and those
who argue that biography primarily leads to deepened
knowledge and awareness of other times and places. Whereas
Erikson's concern is primarily with the inner myth, Tuchman's concern is with the outer myth. Erikson's intent in *Young
Man Luther* is to understand how profound psychological crises
and processes shaped a life and how that life in turn helped
shape a culture. Tuchman's interest, on the other hand, is to
understand a culture through the public experience—the
outer life—of a primary player. Tuchman provides a ratio-

nale for her rejection of the former effort: "Having a strong instinctive sense of privacy myself, I feel no great obligation to pry into a subject's private life."

This conflict, however, should not lead us astray from our immediate goal of determining what and how we learn from biography. Tuchman and Vandiver make the point well: through the study of one life we may learn a great deal about history and culture. Vandiver's biography of Black Jack Pershing is a case in point. Through Pershing's life we learn more about the history and culture of the Great Plains, the western frontier, the Philippines, Mexico, Europe, and South America, as well as a half-century of United States military history. Our knowledge of the history of American foreign policy and the process whereby the United States became a world power is enhanced. We learn about the growth of bureaucracy in a nation come of age, and our knowledge of the changing values and ideals of a culture in transition is deepened.

Through biography we gain knowledge of the universal conditions under which all lives are formed and lived, the conditions of freedom and fate. By fate I mean the limits of circumstance, the conditions of a person's life that can be affirmed or transcended only by choice. One's destiny is forged through the constant interplay between fate and freedom. If freedom is not exercised—choices made—then circumstance becomes the dominant force in a person's life.

It is interesting to speculate on how the kind of biography written in this century—biography that explores the inner myth and its consequence on human behavior—might someday influence our collective understanding and vision of human life. We tend to think that the craft of biography is influenced by seminal thinkers, and it is, but the obverse may be true as well. The use of biographical studies in philosophy, theology, and artistic endeavor remains, by and large, unexplored. In particular, much can be learned about freedom and fate, the two conditions that no life can escape.

Robert Abzug, in his response to Frank Vandiver's paper, provides a preliminary framework for understanding this kind of insight. In reviewing a few successful biographies, Abzug notes that

in each case the author had made me feel at once the presence of the core of his or her subject and the illusion that that subject was yet to be created. . . . In a sense each biographer had created the old Calvinist drama, the struggle between free will and predestination. The universe of the biography became one in which the presupposition of a fate had been reinforced by prefiguring and foreshadowing intrusions, images, and the like; yet the expectation of a life to be relived, with all its turns and accidents, had not been destroyed. Indeed, it had been made more compelling.

Abzug concludes with the provocative statement that "good biography worked for me when it hinted in some quiet way that even as it assayed one life it ritually enacted every life."

All lives evidence the struggle between freedom and fate. Through biography we learn more of the intensity of this struggle; we perceive new dimensions to these most powerful conditions of human existence. In the life of Alice James we see the extent to which a human soul is unable to surmount, despite sometimes heroic efforts, the heavy weight of those forces determining personality. In the life of Abraham Lincoln we see the capacity of a human being to claim the freedom that does exist and to transcend, as much as might be possible, determining influences. Yet for Lincoln as well as James the struggle between freedom and fate was lifelong and peculiarly intense.

Unless the subject is a minor figure about whom we know very little, we begin a biography with a general awareness of the person's life and possibly death. What we do not know, by and large, is the course of the life—the early influences, the psychological dispositions, the weight of a culture, the molding events, and how the individual worked his or her way through, around, and beyond these fateful factors. We learn how the individual succeeded or failed to claim the freedom inherent in human existence, to make fundamental choices affirming or transcending the limits of circumstance.

The struggle between freedom and fate takes place within a context. We are not left to ponder these conditions of human existence without a reference. "Every individual biography," states sociologist Peter Berger, "is an episode within the history of society, which both precedes and survives it." Hence the individual's struggle with freedom and fate takes place within a societal and cultural context. The ideas, values, and institutions of a society influence greatly the individual's self-understanding.

Berger's work in the sociology of knowledge focuses on how we as human beings construct, maintain, change, and discard those fundamental ideas and values that sustain a society. The human community, in its pursuit of order and meaning, creates necessary structures, an objective world of ideas and values that, after a time, comes to confront the individual as a powerful reality separated from its human origins. Order in a society is preserved as long as this objective reality is affirmed by the individual. In periods of great social, cultural, and political turmoil, individuals doubt the truth of this objective reality, and such alienation gives way to new ideas and new values. Creating and sustaining an objective reality is thus an ongoing process.

Berger has an apt metaphor for the objective reality that man creates: the sacred canopy. If this canopy is convincingly in place, the institutions of a society are strong, and fundamental ideas and values are clear. No society, however, can sustain for very long a canopy that does not change. Individuals begin to doubt the prevailing canopy, and new ideas and values are projected onto it.

The fate and freedom that we learn about through biography have as their foundation the sacred canopies of a given time and place. Although one discovers some constants in these canopies, some factors that do not vary from one society to another or one time to another, one is struck by the extent of variance and change. Within our own culture and society one need look only at the biographies of two presidents, Stephen Oates's of Abraham Lincoln and Doris Kearns's of Lyndon Johnson, to see the extent to which the canopy upholding American society and culture changed from the nineteenth to the twentieth century. We see this change through the lives of two American boys who grew up to be president of the United States. The Lincoln and Johnson biographies evidence the subtle changes made in the prevailing American canopy by the communities and families of the subjects. Regional, local, and familial incorporation of certain aspects of the canopy and rejection or disdain of others can be seen. Certain ideas, values, ethics, and institutions are given sacred status in one place but not another, or in one family and not another.

Good biography is dramatic, for we see the struggle between freedom and fate within the context of a sacred canopy. To be born poor and on the frontier in the early years of the Republic is fate; we understand the meaning of this fate—and how Lincoln, in his freedom, responded to it— from the perspective of a society that upholds a canopy that includes specific ideas about the common man, about individualism and success, about honesty and simplicity. To be born in 1908 in a farmhouse alongside the Pedernales River in the Hill Country of Texas, the son of a hard-drinking, domino-playing father and a self-denying, Browning-loving mother, is fate; we understand the power and nature of this fate in the context of Lyndon Johnson's claim on the American dream, on aspirations and ideals rooted in the sacred canopy of twentieth-century America. To be born into the James family of Boston in the mid-nineteenth century is also fate, but the power and dimensions of that fate can be known only by looking at the peculiar Jamesian adaptation of the nineteenth-century American sacred canopy.

Every life story, then, is about an individual's relationship to a sacred canopy. Our journey through life is ultimately a solitary affair, for we are forced to deal with that canopy. We internalize parts of it, making those parts our own, and that contributes to our fate. We reject other parts, and that too is our fate, but, in our human creativity, we exercise our freedom to create our own reality, to change the canopy (with the consequence that our children and grandchildren must struggle with those changes). If the canopy crumbles through our experience, we must endure the confusion of a world that no longer makes sense. Therein lie our freedom and fate as well.

Ronald Steel makes an interesting point about the kind of biography read by this generation: ". . . we seek not reassuring tales of people who conform to society's restrictions but inspiring accounts of those who overcome obstacle and tradition. We are exalted not by lives of the saints but by heroic exploits against great odds and unfeeling bureaucracies." Our penchant for this kind of biography reflects the fact that the sacred canopy of our society is filled with holes. Confused over what is true, right, good, and beautiful, we cast about for stories of people who struggled to find a way—through freedom and fate—to wholeness and purpose. At the same time we are curious about those who fail, those who go mad when "obstacle and tradition" cannot be overcome and "heroic exploits" cannot be undertaken. Here we find the other side of the coin, the path that some follow when the sacred canopy disintegrates. Both types of biography provide lessons, not in morality but in the intense, lonely struggle between freedom and fate.

Two Lives

Biography is a prism of history and also of the human personality, naked and clothed, and of the universal conditions of freedom and fate. Biography is the handmaiden of psychology and philosophy as well as of history.

The kinds of insight gained through biography—knowledge of how people have given shape to their lives, knowledge of other ages and cultures, knowledge of the conditions of freedom and fate—cannot be separated. Good biography and good reading depend upon the imaginative interplay of all three.

This interplay can be seen in the works of the biographers who have contributed to this volume: Robert Abzug, Stephen Oates, Ronald Steel, Jean Strouse, and Frank Vandiver. For the purpose of this paper, however, I would like to concentrate on two biographies, Ronald Steel's *Walter Lippmann* and Jean Strouse's *Alice James*. A brief summary of these lives helps us understand the importance of biography to humanistic inquiry.

In 1955, when he was sixty-six, Walter Lippmann suffered a nervous breakdown, requiring hospitalization and weeks of recuperation. Lippmann provided an explanation: the collapse had been brought on by "trying to swim so long against the current of public opinion." Lippmann added, "Sometimes I wish I had a profession, like law or medicine or chemistry, which has recognizable subject matter and methods." The fundamental human problem of belonging to a profession that is still ill-defined cannot be minimized. Put simply, from the perspective of our earlier frame of reference, Lippmann, for much of his life, stood alone, a professional man whose profession was inadequately grounded in the sacred canopy of American society. One should not be surprised by Lippmann's breakdown after decades of exhausting work. But the reason for the breakdown, according to Lippmann, was not the work but the circumstance that his profession was insufficiently defined and understood.

Yet this most remarkable journalistic career, spanning six decades from 1910 to 1970, helped Americans understand and come to terms with a world that was changing dramatically. Events and processes frequently challenged, undermined, and destroyed various elements of the sacred canopy that held late-nineteenth-century America together: World War I, the Depression, World War II, the Cold War and the reality of annihilation, civil disorder, the tragedy of Vietnam. Lippmann was a voice of reason for millions of Americans, a man of wisdom seeking to make sense out of events and changes that threatened the well-being of our sacred canopy and the society served by that canopy. But Lippmann also provided an interpretation for new ideas, values, and structures that tended to rework and reshape this canopy. With eyes on the future Lippmann was in the business of refurbishing a sacred canopy.

Lippmann's personal life and ideas shared a common characteristic: a continuing search for order, structure, and purpose. Lippmann was not comfortable with the irrational. With the exception of a few years of association with anarchists and revolutionists following his Harvard education, Lippmann shunned eccentricity, rejected iconoclasm, and distrusted emotionalism, while embracing objectivity, stoicism, and abstract intellectualism. Growing maturity and World War I transformed the young Lippmann, the author of the progressive *A Preface to Politics* (1913), into the serious, ascetic, and objective journalist and philosopher of *A Preface To Morals* (1929).

Lippmann's work, grounded in a quest for order, helped legitimate the changing nature of the sacred canopy under which Americans lived, worked, played, and died. Steel hints at this when he states that Lippmann "had a remarkable facility for not straying too far from the main thrust of public opinion." Lippmann took that opinion, sometimes rough and embryonic, and made sense out of it: "When the dominant mood was progressivist, he was a progressive; when it was for intervention, he was a Wilsonian idealist; when it was disillusioned, he was the skeptic of *Public Opinion* and *A Preface To Morals*; when it was for social change, he embraced FDR's experiments." He was not, however, a propagandist or an echoer of opinion. When he fought for Roosevelt's program, for instance, it was to give content to nascent ideas and to sharpen proposed solutions to pressing problems.

Occasionally, however, Lippmann challenged the sacred canopy of his time, questioning fundamental assumptions, values, and attitudes. To some extent, his denial of a traditional religious faith and his affirmation of secular humanism involved a rejection of some important elements in the sacred canopy of Western civilization. More important, his intellectual integrity, his willingness to confront the canopy when necessary, can be seen in a number of major issues with which he dealt, especially issues related to the early years of the Cold War. Going against the grain, he argued that the increasing militancy of the United States government should be denounced. Rejecting both the idealists, who believed that world law and international parliaments would preserve the peace, and the interventionists, who preached United States military influence worldwide, Lippmann offered, in two books published in 1943 and in his many newspaper columns, an alternative: a political accord between the Soviet Union and the United States based on mutual recognition of the need for security. Peace lay in great-power cooperation; just as Russia cannot deny our sphere of influence in Latin America, so we cannot deny Russia's sphere of influence in eastern Europe. As United States foreign policy sought more and more to contain communism through United States military presence worldwide, Lippmann argued against specific policy decisions of the United States, including the crusade in Turkey and Greece to suppress Communist-led rebellions, the division of Germany into two nations and the rearmament of "our" Germany, and military support for Chiang Kai-shek. What Lippmann feared ultimately happened: the dissipation of American strength and morality as the United States bolstered discredited governments in regions around the world where it had no vested interests, including Vietnam. For Lippmann, United States foreign policy had lost sight of rational objectives.

One finds in the biography a tension between Lippmann's legitimating, even with modification, certain political and social facets of the sacred canopy of twentieth-century America and his occasional challenges to such facets. Steel points out that Lippmann "felt an insider's responsibility for making the system work. He was never alienated and was in no sense a radical. He operated entirely within the system." Yet he constantly pressed beyond political platforms, bureaucratic practices, and administrative policies to the real and inherently more important values and ideas that would preserve a democratic society and maintain world order. In this process Lippmann sometimes seemed the troublemaker, the destroyer of images, persons, and policies.

Lippmann's personal life bears a strong resemblance to his intellectual life. A man of great discipline, he followed a schedule that simply could not be broken. He was, says Steel, "a person accustomed to having what he wanted." His personal life-style was so morally correct that he endured a twenty-year emotionally and intellectually barren marriage. Lippmann thought about divorce, but he did not want to be the agent of excessive pain or the recipient of hate and rejection. Instead, he withdrew and concentrated on his work; indeed, his many associations seemed to lack emotional involvement. Operating under a set of given principles and ideas, Lippmann assumed a peculiar stoicism.

All of this changed in 1937, when, at the age of forty-eight, Lippmann fell in love with the wife of one of his few close friends. For the first time in his life Lippmann was able to let go, to break through his loneliness and sense of propriety to embrace the irrationality of passionate love, whatever the cost. He divorced his wife, giving her all his financial assets, and married his lover. A new optimism and confidence emerged. In his newfound passion he could put aside the opinions and ethics of the world, and, though he worked to minimize the pain the divorce and remarriage brought to the other partners and to his colleagues, he gave in to the happiness of love.

As much as Walter Lippmann was a public person, Alice James was a private person. While Lippmann was consumed with the political content of the twentieth-century American canopy, Alice James was preoccupied with the psychological realities of the late-nineteenth-century canopy. Living was extraordinarily difficult for Alice, for she had to deal as a woman not only with the larger cultural canopy but also with the peculiar adjustments the James family made to this objectivated reality.

Jean Strouse writes that "though Alice's life can be seen in several contexts—including the history of nineteenth-century women, the science of nervous disorders, and the literature of the private life—it was in the family group that she lived with greatest intensity." The family "constituted a self-consciously 'special case,' self-enclosed and self-referring." Independently wealthy, the James family (Henry, Sr.; Mary; and five children—William; Henry, Jr.; Alice; Garth Wilkinson; and Robertson) lived by virtue of a canopy within a canopy. Henry, Sr., the strong father, never held a conventional job; he spent his life "in pursuit of religious truth" and in support of his family's intellectual and cultural quest. Henry, Sr., while rejecting much of New England Calvinism, nevertheless retained a good deal of the Puritan spirit, and the story of Alice James is a story of one unable to come to terms with that Jamesian interpretation of the meaning and nature of life.

"Most families," writes Strouse, "generate myths about themselves, but few place the kind of premium the Jameses did on simultaneously reinforcing the myths and presenting private perceptions of truth for public consumption." At the heart of the James family myth, as Alice grew up, was a peculiar twist on the old Calvinist notion of the importance of success. Henry, Sr., endorsed a "strenuous individualism that stressed being extraordinary no matter what one chose actually to do" in life. The inner life was far more important than the outer life, says Strouse, and success "had nothing to do with the temporal rewards of laurels, lucre, and fame," but lay in perception and the ability to communicate a "sense of self that had to do with a quality of being and the ability to see life steadily (as Matthew Arnold put it) and see it whole."

This Jamesian understanding of success was achieved by two of the four sons, Henry, Jr., and William. The objectivated reality of nineteenth-century America presented many problems for women—as seen in the growing protest movement toward the end of the century—but the peculiar interpretation and shaping of this reality in the James family made the challenge of living doubly difficult for Alice. Strouse quotes Henry, Jr.: "In our family group girls seem scarcely to have had a chance." Strouse adds that "to be a James and a girl . . . was a contradiction in terms." The story of Alice James is one of intense "struggle to resolve that essential contradiction."

It is difficult to imagine anyone struggling harder and suffering more to resolve the contradiction than did Alice James. While her nervous susceptibility can be seen at an early age—at age fourteen, says Strouse, Alice concluded that life for her meant renunciation—she did not suffer a total collapse until 1868, when she was nineteen. Strouse describes the most fundamental dilemma faced by Alice. She was caught between two impossibilities: identifying with her father and brothers, on the one hand, and with her mother and aunt, on the other. "To use her mind productively would have meant entering the lists in competition with Henry, William, and Henry, Sr." To compete with men, despite her abundant intelligence and proclivity, she found inappropriate and impossible. Thus, every time Alice began to do intellectual work, attacks of hysteria followed. But to give in to being the self-sacrificing, self-renouncing woman, as her mother and aunt had, was also impossible, for "turning in that direction would have required Alice to relinquish her sense of superior intelligence and her desire to be something more than her mother and aunt."

Alice's escape was illness. Although there were periods during the next twenty-four years when her health was more normal and she found partial outlets for her intelligence and creativity—such as teaching history with the progressive Society to Encourage Studies at Home—her life was dominated by illness and by her attempt to make sense of that illness. Strouse writes that Alice's illness "provided her with an escape route—a way out of having to choose between a safe boring life of devotion to others and a dangerous assertion of intellectual competence." It also "justified her failure to achieve while allowing her to preserve a sense of potent capacity." As Alice moved into middle age, her career as an invalid took on other meanings as well. Her illness, which increasingly involved somatic symptoms, was a form of self-assertion, with power cast over family and doctors, all of whom were unable to help. It was also a way of ensuring that she would be cared for, that someone would be looking after her, that she would not be alone in the world.

At the age of forty, three years before her death, Alice, as her illness intensified, arrived at a Jamesian solution—partial as it was—to her struggle, the keeping of a diary:

All of her life Alice had needed an outlet for her energy and ideas. Now, at the age of forty, she found a form that suited her purposes. A diary is private, making no claim as a sort of art or an intellectual argument. She could have it all her own way because "it" was simply experience—her experience—and no objective standard could measure or condemn it. In the privacy of her own journal, she could feel safe from the kind of withering judgment George Eliot had made about the "feminine incapacity for literature," as well as from the criticism she might anticipate from her brothers. The anomalous literary realm occupied by the diary lay safely within the feminine province of the personal; Alice took no overt risk of appearing to compete either with men or with successful women like Eliot.

Alice died of cancer in 1892. Strouse notes that Henry's novels, William's psychology, and Alice's invalidism were careers that grew out of "moral concerns and personal conflicts." "All three careers," says Strouse, "expressed private experience, but two addressed themselves to the world and were crowned with public success, whereas Alice's work affected only herself—and by anybody's standards, a life of incapacitating illness denoted failure and waste." Yet here was her genius, and here was a way out. Illness and failure became, in the last years of her life, the "raw material" of life. "Failure was a bedrock human experience she could claim as her own. An expert at suffering, she could *convert* the waste of her life into something more lasting than private unhappiness." The diary thus became the means for a partial trimph of will over matter, freedom over fate. Born a James, Alice died a James.

Understanding

Our understanding of human life is enriched by knowing Walter Lippmann and Alice James. We see contrasting lives in their totality. We see beginnings, endings, and quests in between.

We learn much about nineteenth- and twentieth-century history and culture through these two lives. In Lippmann, a public person who gave the world twenty-three books, several hundred articles, and several thousand editorials and newspaper columns, we find a journey though nearly all the major events and developments of this century. We see the behind-the-scenes activity of a single man and his associates, observers, and participants in twentieth-century American history. Lippmann's relationship to Lyndon Johnson, for instance, leads to a deeper perspective on the American political scene of the 1960s. Lippmann's feeling that he had been betrayed by Johnson is symbolic of the American public's feeling of betrayal over broken campaign pledges. In Alice James we find a person who leads us to the remnants of Puritanism in nineteenth-century New England; to the intellectual elite of Boston; to the social, economic, and cultural status of American women in the nineteenth century; to the history of medicine and psychology. At a more particular level, one sees the impact of the Civil War on a family's identity, provoking crises of both masculinity and femininity. William's description of Alice as an "idle and useless young female" describes prevailing male attitudes and the plight of thousands of Alices.

But we learn much more than this, for we gain insight into human psychology by knowing how Alice James and Walter Lippmann gave shape to their lives. We see, as Leon Edel says, the inner myths. The various meanings that Alice gave to her illness provide the key to her perception of herself. Some of these meanings were gleaned from prevailing cultural myths. "Illness," writes Strouse, "made women ethereal and interesting." As understood by Alice, illness was an expression of mid-Victorian ideas of femininity. Women were by nature delicate, and "a graceful languor, pallor, and vulnerability" went with the ideal of beauty. Nervousness, a particular illness, was also seen as characteristic of women with intelligence, sensitivity, and shyness. Finally, one finds the incorporation of the "bank account theory" of health: the James family was entitled to just so much good health, and the intense suffering of one would ensure that sufficient resources were left to others. By exploring these and other perceptions of illness, one begins to understand the inner myth by which Alice James lived, suffered, and died.

It is possible that the sheer weight of Lippmann's intellectual productivity can overshadow the inner myths by which he lived. The strength of Steel's biography rests in part, however, on the extent to which he demonstrates the connection between Lippmann's life and ideas and his perceptions of himself, his inner myths. In spite of his accomplishments, his apparent self-confidence, his associations with the movers and shakers of his age, and his influence on twentieth-century history, Lippmann was insecure and vulnerable. His aloofness, even coldness, and his sense of isolation were clearly recognized by Lippmann; in fact, he seemed to turn these weaknesses into strengths as America's most eminent journalist. Whether it was a contributing cause or an expression of this problem, one finds in the early Lippmann consuming ambivalence over his Jewishness. As anti-Semitism grew in the 1920s, Lippmann was forced, privately and publicly, to come to terms with his identity. In response to the question whether Harvard University should limit the enrollment of Jews, Lippmann provided, says Steel, "a masterpiece of equivocation" based on his own ambivalence. Lippmann was disturbed, he said, by the "distressing personal and social habits" of Jews brought on "by a bitter history and intensified by a pharisaical theology." Lippmann refused throughout his life to belong to or identify with Jewish organizations. Jews must not be ostentatious or conspicuous; they should identify with the wider culture and society. Assimiliation is the goal. Lippmann, while not denying his Jewishness, never spoke about it, and his associates avoided the subject. Steel notes, "In rejecting, or at least circumnavigating, his Jewishness, Lippmann had to deny a part of himself." Lippmann learned to conceal his vulnerability. Through choices affecting his career, subject matter, and associations, Lippmann successfully protected himself during a very long life. The extent to which this quest robbed him of the potential for deep and lasting friendship, derived from sharing one's most vulnerable self with others, can only be surmised.

In addition to these kinds of contributions that the two biographies make to our insight into life, the ultimate contribution comes to us, as Robert Abzug says, through the ritual enactment of every life. Lippmann and James are two very different players in the universal drama of human life. We see the nature of the sacred canopy under which they lived, the power of ideas, attitudes, institutions, and collective self-understanding. We see what they inherited, what they accommodated to, and what they sought to change. We see what was "given" to them, what they did with that which was given, and what they left behind.

Above all, we come to see the meaning of freedom and fate. Being born a Jew in New York City in 1889 or being born a female member of the James family in 1848 is fate; helping to found the *New Republic* or making sense out of one's invalid life through the keeping of a diary is freedom. All lives are shaped by the creative tension between freedom and fate, and good biography gives us a peculiar and special vision of the nature of this tension and the consequence on individual lives and, for public persons, on society as well.

We gain a sense of lives well lived or not so well lived. We learn a lot about dispositions, influences, values, controlling ideas, prejudices, fears, and the power of institutions. But we also learn a lot about risk, creativity, good luck, brilliance, and fortitude. We learn about suffering, failure, and death, and we learn about happiness, success, and rebirth.

What we see are lives lived under sacred canopies, whether such canopies are complete, powerful, and assuring or disintegrated, impotent, and troubling. Like the chorus of a Sophoclean play, we participate in the unfolding drama, projecting onto the story our understanding of the life being told, our assessment of the life being lived. But when the weekend is over and the biography is read, the tear that we shed is as much over our life as it is over the one whom we have come to know. We suck in our gut and go about our business, but we know more about that mysterious canopy and about the limits of circumstance and the awesomeness of choice. We are not given answers, only insight.

Frank Vandiver makes a telling point: persistence is the essence of humanism. When Alice James, in the last years of her illness-ridden life, takes up the pen and writes the first line on the first page of a small leather-bound volume in order to give meaning to her experience, we learn about persistence. When we see Walter Lippmann, a frail, totally exhausted man of eighty-four, manage to leave his bed in a nursing home to walk, with the aid of only his crutches, down the aisle of a New York Unitarian church for the funeral service of his beloved wife, we learn about human persistence. "Shockingly thin, his fine cheekbones protruding under his flaccid skin, his black suit hanging loosely on his emaciated frame, he seemed terribly alone—a solitary and immensely courageous figure."

Like Lippmann, we meet fate solitarily. With Walter Lippmann, Alice James, Theodore Weld, Abraham Lincoln, John Pershing, Martin Luther King, Jr., and many others, we may be able to meet fate with courage. Therein lies our freedom. Therein lies the gift and beauty of good biography.

Conversations

JOE HOLLEY WITH ROBERT H. ABZUG

HOLLEY: I begin with an obvious question: What are the characteristics of good biography?

ABZUG: I was thinking earlier not so much what makes a good biography as what needs, whether they are cultural or personal, biographies fulfill. Why are they perpetually being written? Why are they so popular with the general reader? What is it about recounted lives that is so particularly appealing, whether they are famous or almost famous or in one way or another touch on the world of history or literature? And I was thinking about the biographers participating in the Texas Lecture and Institute on the Humanities—the enormous variety of books. You have Ronald Steel writing about Walter Lippmann, a very important newspaper columnist, and my own work on Theodore Weld, a nineteenth-century abolitionist. You have Jean Strouse, who has written about an invalid who does nothing, and that's the basis of her story. And yet that's compelling and important.

HOLLEY: Would it have been important if Alice James's brothers had also done nothing?

ABZUG: I think that Jean Strouse would certainly make the case, and I would make it, that, if you masked out the fame of her father and her brothers—the James Gang—the story of her struggle as a woman in the late nineteenth century would be intrinsically interesting. Lincoln's importance is obvious. Stephen Oates's challenge was to enter a field already overwritten and offer something new. There must be more biographies and miscellany on Lincoln than on any other American public figure. He is so important on so many levels and is so mythic, in a way, that he can be constantly reinvestigated. And then Frank Vandiver's work on Pershing, a military figure, is important for other reasons.

So there are many reasons for writing biography. I remember a similar discussion with a fellow graduate student at Berkeley years ago. Why write biography, and why particularly psychobiography? It always struck me as an important point that in an age without heroes—everybody bemoans the fact that there are no heroes; it has become a cliché—an age when particular well-known individuals don't play the old symbolic role of the hero, biography does play an important role in showing that great people who achieve a certain amount in the world—whether in terms of inner struggles and resolutions or leaving great wills in politics or art or whatever—experience the pains and conflicts that impinge on all our lives. In other words, one task of modern biography at its best has been to bring common people, the readers, into a closer awareness and understanding of how much great persons, great by accident or by genius or by hard work, share in common humanity with them. Psychoanalytic biography at its best certainly contributes to this perspective.

HOLLEY: Is it the psychoanalytic approach itself that offers these insights into the individual?

ABZUG: I think it offers one route. I think it's clear that great literature offers these insights. If you go back to the nineteenth century and read Tolstoy, Eliot, or Flaubert or any of the great psychological novelists, the inner life of people is all there without psychoanalysis. What psychoanalysis adds in some ways is not the psychoanalytic jargon but the proposition that the unconscious and certain ways that the unconscious is formed have a deep influence, a formative influence, on all lives, and therefore any explanation or a description of a life should be couched in some way that takes the unconscious into account.

HOLLEY: How accurate are the clues, particularly for someone who lived a hundred and fifty years ago?

ABZUG: Well, in some ways they are very accurate. If, for instance, you are lucky and you have a fair run of letters, diaries, whatever, from a person's life, and you see a person live and die and have some perspective on an entire life-span and have enough perspective to see and to shape a world around that life, you have a lot more than a psychoanalyst has when he sees a patient four or five hours a week in an analytic situation. There are certain things that the psycho-historian does not have that the analyst does have.

I think the best defense of any work of history is the cumulative or total effect of one's reading of that work. Does the interpretation make sense? Do we really know that this or another was the only motivation? A bad psychohistorian says that this and only this is why someone did something. That's the kind of reductionism that people attack and rightly so. But I don't think that invalidates having a multiple description and analysis of a person's motivations in the world that includes a layer of psychoanalytic explanation.

That was in fact what I was trying to do with *Passionate Liberator*. It's an orthodox historical work in many ways, but I felt that for an eccentric like Weld, when one's sense of his world and his life and his inner self could be amplified by asking questions about what *might* be going on underneath it all, I asked those questions. But I don't think that *Passionate Liberator* ever relies simply on the psychoanalytic explanation, largely because that explanation goes nowhere.

Some of the usual criticisms that can be made are that if you are writing psychobiographies of males they will all go through oedipal crises, they will all have struggles with their fathers, they will all have yearnings after their mothers, and they will all have all sorts of conflicts that are right out of the textbook. So what have you shown? You have made them case studies of a theory rather than persons in history. That's bad psychobiography. But, like anything else, there is good and bad. What I was looking for, and I can only speak for myself, was an added dimension.

HOLLEY: What did Erikson teach you and other psycho-biographers?

ABZUG: It's an interesting question because I have lived with Erikson's work for sixteen or seventeen years. I read *Young Man Luther* when I was a sophomore in college, and I was very angry at it. I didn't like psychoanalysis then. In fact, I had a very telling reaction. Obviously, there was some appeal to me. I still have the original copy, and I noticed the things that I underlined, and they are the parts of the book that now greatly appeal to me. So, in other words, I was keyed in to the very same things. There was something appealing and gripping about the book. I have always had mixed feelings about Erikson's work as a historian.

On the one hand, just the fact that Erikson dared write that book—and *Gandhi's Truth*, his other psychobiography—is important. He took the dare. He went ahead and did psychobiography in a sympathetic way, in a way that had not been done before. My mixed feelings come from the fact that the Luther and Gandhi books are more case studies in psychoanalysis than history. They are fine as that, but as history I always felt that they are not good models. It seems to me that the real work of a psychohistorian is to do his work fully and completely on both sides of that hyphen—well, it's no longer hyphenated—the two sides of that word—to be the psychoanalyst, but most of all to be the historian. To know, for instance, how much a part accident plays in history, how much a part class and region and conscious decisions play in the formation of a historical character, but by no means forgetting, and boldly going into, the psyche for an added dimension.

HOLLEY: How did you get interested in Theodore Dwight Weld?

ABZUG: I was doing work on abolitionism and was perusing Weld's published letters looking for evidence for an article. I came across his love letters to Angelina Grimke, whom he later married. They were so impassioned and so revealing and so touching that I became enthralled with his character. I was interested, in other words, in the coming of the Civil War, in southern history, in reform history—the whole antebellum era—and here was a person who came alive in these letters.

HOLLEY: What is the practical process of getting at the resources you need to find who Theodore Dwight Weld actually was?

ABZUG: It's a normal kind of research procedure. You first read everything that has been written; you scour every bibliographical device known to the reference librarian to find out what has been written about him, about the time, about everything. Then through various means you find out where the major collections of manuscripts are—letters, diaries, manuscripts of all kinds—and then you begin the real research, which in my case meant moving from Berkeley to Boston for two years. I used Boston as a base to spend time in Ann Arbor, Michigan, in the Clements Library. I spent months in Ann Arbor, on and off, photocopying letters and doing the gut research from the basic Weld collection. There were large holdings at the Boston Public Library, at Harvard University, and at the Massachusetts Historical Society. I also made trips to New York to the New York Historical Society, to the Library of Congress in Washington, to the Western Reserve Historical Society in Cleveland, to Columbus, to Cincinnati. I spent about a year and a half to two years just researching. And it wasn't only Weld. In order to understand Weld, you have to understand just about every major figure in the abolitionist movement. Not all of that comes through in *Passionate Liberator*; otherwise, it would have been a multi-volume work on all the abolitionists.

HOLLEY: When you are doing that kind of basic research, are there motivating questions in your mind for which you are seeking answers?

ABZUG: There are questions you begin with, and then there are questions that arise. There are also those wonderful moments when you are bored stiff after reading the fiftieth letter of some year, and all of a sudden a sentence or a phrase or a particular letter makes everything come together or suggests such a totally new theme and such a totally new insight to a person that you walk around in a daze, because it has become your life. You begin to live this person's life.

There is also a stage in writing a biography in which you move into an identification with the person. Some people never move out of it; I have, thank God, but there is this process of being yourself and then merging with this figure in some way and then realizing that you can't write about him if you are merged with him. So you move toward some midway point in empathy and connection but also dispassion.

Holley: Do you have to like him?

Abzug: No. I would hate to think that all those Hitler biographers like him. I think you have to be fascinated by the person, and probably because that person has some theme, some element, of you in him. Just like people you meet. Some people leave you totally cold, others annoy you, others you find fascinating but dangerous, and still others you feel really comfortable with. It's the same way with historical figures, once you get to know them. In the case of Weld, I at first liked him, then I grew to dislike certain parts of him, and then I gained a deep respect for the man that overarched petty gripes that I had with the way he lived his life.

Holley: Were you sometimes disappointed in Weld as his life unfolded? Did you wish he had done something else, either for the biography's sake or because you were interested in the man?

Abzug: There were all those quandaries. There were times—at least this was my experience—when I had a double reaction. I was disappointed in what he had done in a certain situation—for instance, in his marriage—on the other hand, as a writer, historian, and biographer, it gave me a chance to put some distance between myself and the man. It gave me a chance to put some criticism into a generally sympathetic work, to show that I was really telling the whole story, not just being his advocate at the court of history. As always, you have mixed feelings.

Holley: As his biographer, were you disappointed that Weld left the stage of history, literally lost his voice and became a private person?

Abzug: I think that's going to be an ongoing question with me, simply because when I initially went into the work my sense was that I was disappointed—a sense that "my God, it's 1844! We have a whole sixteen years before the war; what are you doing?"

Holley: And he has another fifty years to live.

Abzug: Yes, that's the fascinating thing about him. He's famous in less than half of his life, and later lives in a fashion that he himself respects much more.

One of the challenges in writing this biography of a man who lived to be ninety-odd years, and who lived so many lives, who was constantly meeting difficulties and coming through, is that, especially in the period I was doing the research and writing—in my own personal life, in the life of the nation—the whole world seemed rather fragile. That was 1971 to 1974. Just one thing after the next—Vietnam, Watergate, the oil crisis, and various Watergates and Vietnams in my own life. It's a marvelous thing to be writing a biography of a man who has experienced not similar things but things similar in tone—life changes, tragedy, disaster, whatever—and just watch him go on and on and on. I was very glad I wasn't writing a biography of Keats or Shelley or Mozart, all of whom lived rather short lives. There was a way in which Weld was a very quiet inspiration. It wasn't necessarily what he did; it was the doggedness with which he kept on reevaluating his life, whatever the decisions or the ideas. I'm hardly a pietistic Christian, but here was a man of inner questioning; he constantly reevaluated, and was able to do so for a period of close to a century. Now that's inspirational when you're in the midst of a personal world and a public world that seem in total flux. So in addition to his being my friend and subject and object he was something else to me during that time. But I began to distance myself from that after a time. I became conscious of this role model, and then Weld became demythologized.

HOLLEY: Was there a point in your getting to know Mr. Weld that you knew him so well and you knew so much about him that you began to feel that there was no way you could translate all that into a book?

ABZUG: I went through a number of different stages. I never felt that it would be worthwhile to write from my early knowledge of Weld because that would simply be repeating the earlier biography of the man. That might have been a temptation had there been no other biography. There was a point in my research when I had learned so much and knew so many particular aspects of Weld's life that I was no longer sure how these particulars related to the total life. He became such a complex figure that, even if I had a thousand pages to write, I wasn't sure what I wanted to say. There was a point at which all that material had to simmer, and I had to think things through—consciously, unconsciously, let things sift, work on something else.

HOLLEY: Did Weld's peculiar personality contribute to that problem?

ABZUG: Every biographer undoubtedly experiences that difficult time, but Weld's strange character certainly intensified the problem for me. One of the characteristics I hope people sense from *Passionate Liberator* is that this book doesn't come to a lot of specific conclusions, largely because I finally felt that, at least for Weld, the most important biographical task would be to redescribe his life. I didn't begin with a long agenda of historiographical questions. Other historians had asked the question, "Who was more important, Weld or Garrison?" By the time I finished researching the book, that was a meaningless question to me. What I wanted to say about Weld wasn't going to be a simple historiographical point. Rather, he would be a medium through which I would describe in a way that had not quite been described and in a depth that had not been reached in other works about most other reformers, a new sense of the reform experience in America and the personal experience of reform.

I am not necessarily saying that every reformer did this or that; the intent became less to answer specific questions and more to describe a life in history in a way that would make it personally compelling and would also tell us something about how people get involved in radical movements—the questions that those movements are answering in their lives, what meaning they have for them, how they change, and how their commitments change with those changes in their lives. That's what I would say *Passionate Liberator* is all about. You couldn't list the answers; that wouldn't be a satisfactory way of looking at this book—though it is a satisfactory way of looking at some other very good biographies and certainly of other kinds of histories. This was an attempt to do justice to the intricacies, the emotions, the quandaries, the conflicts of a nineteenth-century life in its own terms.

HOLLEY: How is your book different from the earlier Weld biography?

ABZUG: Benjamin Thomas's *Theodore Dwight Weld: Crusader for Freedom* is a public biography that concentrates on Weld's public life, his life as an organizer. I felt the need to find out what made the man tick. Thomas's is a heroic biography in the traditional sense.

I don't lack awe for the man, but I guess I see some of his virtues differently. I see more virtue in his constant self-scrutiny than I do in his charismatic speeches on the hustings. So there is a different aesthetic and a different value sense about what is important. I find great importance in his relationship with Angelina Grimke. I think Thomas spends literally half the number of pages that I do on their relationship.

HOLLEY: I was wondering if that relationship was known to the Welds' contemporaries or to Thomas.

ABZUG: It was known but not considered important. It was considered kind of cute—admirable in some ways, but not as important as the central issue of slavery and his changing vision of the world. My emphasis is heretical in some ways. Some of the reviewers who have liked the book very much are surprised that so much weight is given to the personal life, not only the marriage but the spiritual cravings and all the rest. They talk about it as a radical departure, and I'm happy about that because I like to think that I produced a book that is a little different.

HOLLEY: Do you see yourself as Robert Abzug, biographer, or Robert Abzug, historian, or both?

ABZUG: I think it was very important for me—personally, selfishly—to do the Weld biography. I'm interested in many other questions, and the projects that are on the burners are not biographical. Having worked in biography, having worked in a psychoanalytic-biographical mode, you never see the world quite the same again. You understand that these people you are describing, the moments you are analyzing, are not simply ciphers on a chessboard. They are all distinct individuals with their own special personalities, and there are sometimes a lot of problems deciding how to do justice to that sense of individuality when you have set yourself a task other than biography. These historical actors have a biographical dimension, even though that is not what you are interested in at the moment. Somehow you have to do justice to that. I will always be a biographer in spirit, but I am not sure when I will write another biography.

GEOFFREY RIPS WITH RONALD STEEL

RIPS: Why write biography and not history? What are the advantages of biography and the disadvantages?

STEEL: The disadvantages are that you have to stick to somebody's life and events that really happened. That's much more limiting in a way than writing history because in history you reinvent the past, which is not to say that you distort events that really happened. You can, however, choose what events you want to emphasize, and you can write about those events at the expense of others. It gives you great freedom. You rearrange the past.

With biography you don't have quite that freedom. Somebody's life determines the emphasis. You can choose to put a certain weight on an aspect of a person's life, but you also have to deal with certain things that are very real. You can't decide, for example, that a person's parents were insignificant just because you want them to be insignificant. If the person is a writer, you have to deal with his major writings even if those writings don't interest you. As a historian, I don't think you have to do that to quite that degree. You have to deal with these events as they are determined for you.

The advantage of writing biography, however, is the obvious personal aspect, in that it allows you to approach events through a certain perspective. Otherwise, it's confusion; it's difficult to decide how to approach an issue. You have to approach it through some kind of framework. Some people write history through the framework of an ideological lens, or they use an arbitrary date, or they do great battles, or they want to prove a thesis. Biography gives you a framework in which to view events.

Many biographies aren't history. Many are character studies, and the history is a secondary aspect. In my own case— the case of Walter Lippmann—I thought biography was a very useful way of approaching the great events of history that he witnessed. His life seemed to be indistinguishable from his times, since he spent his entire life commenting on the times. If I were to set out to do a history of the times that he wrote about, I'd have to write a history of the twentieth century. First, I didn't want to write a history of the twentieth century. Second, it's been done. And third, what framework would you use? I used Lippmann as a framework, if you will, because he chose to cover certain events. He chose to cover events not just because he was interested in them but because they were important. That was his job. He was paid to write about what was important. Therefore, if he didn't deal with an event, either he sincerely believed it wasn't important or he sincerely didn't want to write about it even though it was important. Why he didn't want to write about it then becomes a biographical consideration. The two become mixed and in a way reinforce each other.

RIPS: So, in choosing your subject, you wouldn't have chosen to write about someone who didn't have this great interaction with historic events?

STEEL: Well, I might choose to write somebody's biography, but I wouldn't necessarily feel it was history. You could write a biography of Auden, for example, and it wouldn't be history at all, except maybe as backdrop. It would depend upon the life of the subject. I think it would be very difficult to write a biography of Wagner, for example, in which history didn't play a very important role. On the other hand, you could possibly write a biography of Jerome Kern in which it didn't play much of a role at all. The choice of a subject is determined by the biographer's interests. You write a biography of someone who interests you because of the kind of life he or she led. In my case Walter Lippmann interested me because he wrote about events that interested me. I think there is always the element of history in biography, but the degree to which you want to emphasize it depends, even more than on the subject, on the author. You could write a biography of Walter Lippmann, if you wanted to, without confronting a lot of history. You could turn it into a psychobiography. In a way, that's possibly more fun. It gives you a lot of freedom to speculate.

RIPS: I was going to ask you about the use of psychoanalytic theory in biography. Since Lippmann was one of the first to link psychology to politics, in his early writing, I thought it was curious that you seem to eschew any kind of psychological examination of Lippmann.

STEEL: Well, Lippmann did it only for a moment. He was marvelously adept at adopting an idea and milking it, for whatever use it gave him, and then dropping it. He applied certain Freudian concepts, such as repression, to politics in a rather spurious but imaginative way. I don't think he ever applied it to his own life or to politics beyond that foray as a very young man.

You are quite right. I do eschew psychoanalysis—not that I don't think it can be very useful in explaining the behavior of people. I've read some wonderful psychoanalytic biographies, those of Erik Erikson and Alexander and Juliette George's study of Woodrow Wilson and Colonel House. I think Freud's own biography of Wilson is not a good example of that. But I personally don't feel competent to do it. I don't know much about psychoanalysis, and I would be very loath to try to psychoanalyze somebody I hardly know. I think it would be presumptuous on my part. But perhaps someone who knows his subject as little as I know mine personally but who was skilled in psychoanalytic technique would be able to do it. I thought Jean Strouse's biography of Alice James was quite wonderful in the way she dealt with that. Then I've read books that I thought were not very well informed. When it's done well, it can be wonderfully illuminating. In my own case, I had a lot of facts about Lippmann's life, and I did have some ideas about what it all meant. I didn't feel hesitant in presenting those ideas, but I did feel that that was one way of interpreting his life, but I wasn't sure that was the only way. I wanted to let the reader judge, though I did let him know, in some cases, that this was the way it looked to me and maybe that's right and maybe it's not. The more I studied him, the more impressed I was by how little we can know another person.

RIPS: When you choose a subject for biography, do you have specific questions, and do you find the right subject for exploring those questions?

STEEL: That never happened in my case. I was intrigued by the subject: the idea of doing a biography of Walter Lippmann, a man I admired enormously and was greatly influenced by. It was a great opportunity to get at the meaning of certain events. That's why I did it. It's not that I had certain things I wanted to do and then shopped around for somebody to write about. The life and the times intrigued me.

RIPS: So, if you were most interested in how this life intersected certain events, then you wouldn't be interested in psychobiography.

STEEL: In my own case, I am more interested in how it intersected certain events than how people solved certain problems of life.

RIPS: Did you form a greater attachment to your subject as you wrote and did that make it more difficult to be analytical?

STEEL: I certainly formed a great attachment. Unlike the other four biographers in the Texas Institute, I knew my subject and had a personal attachment to him, though not a strong one. He was not the kind of person to whom it was easy to draw near. He wasn't cold or cruel; he was just detached. He was always polite but distant. So, on the personal level, I'm obviously a little more attached to him, but I never felt emotionally involved with him in any way. I didn't feel protective. On the intellectual level—as I learned more about him, his life and career expanded enormously for me, and I discovered aspects of it that I had never before known existed. The complexity of it became more and more fascinating to me, and I became more involved from that point of view. I was fascinated by how it all worked out and how he made sense of it, how he pulled it together. It became an intellectual puzzle. I drew very close to him in that sense.

Another aspect is the identification one makes, in either a positive or a negative sense, as the author with the subject. It becomes a question of to what degree you see yourself in this person. Does the subject's life connect with yours, or do you see his or her life through your own? I discovered a lot of identification in my own case with Lippmann. I don't mean only in a sense of Lippmann's accomplishments but in terms of some of his neuroses, too. There were things about Lippmann that I didn't like that I don't appreciate in myself either. I thought I really understood a lot about him because I identified with him in a curious way that I never expected to when I began this project. I thought I could understand why he did things in a certain way because I would have, or would have been tempted to, at least. I could be wrong about it in that regard, but it really did seem to ring true in a number of ways. So I saw, in a private rather than public way, a lot that I could identify with in Lippmann. I was probably harsher on him than some people might have been precisely because of that.

RIPS: I was thinking of the chapter in the book in which you discuss Lippmann's support of the Republicans during FDR's second election campaign. Near the end of that you seemed to be impassioned on both sides of the issue. You were passionate about the fact that he may have been supporting the Republicans for the wrong reasons. At the same time, you passionately defended him by saying he was hooked on a kind of eighteenth-century liberalism.

STEEL: I probably had mixed feelings about it. I did admire him enormously and still do, and I was surprised by some of the critics who said that I obviously didn't like him very much. I didn't feel that at all. By pointing out some of his foibles, I didn't mean to diminish him in any way. I saw it as an aspect of the complexity of his personality. The way in which he often handled problems was not always admirable, but it was not incomprehensible.

Jeanne Hopkins Stover

with Stephen B. Oates

STOVER: What role does biography play in reconstructing the past?

OATES: The best biography, true biography, seeks to particularize the past, to humanize it, to bring it to life, to impart a sense of real people involved with real issues in an everyday world full of hate and love and laziness, full of stress, full of accomplishments and failures. So I'd say it is to particularize human life—to get away from the abstractions and away from the group generalizations that characterize our fellow disciplines in the social sciences.

STOVER: Would you say that biography in any way dismisses or reinforces myths we have about people in society?

OATES: As a student of biography, I'll simply say this: I think that biography in this country, and perhaps some of the biography written in France and England, has tended to perpetuate the myths that society has held about great people, particularly great men in the American past. I think of Carl Sandburg's Abraham Lincoln. Sandburg's "life" captured the mythical Lincoln more consistently and lyrically than any other biography. So biography can have a tendency to reinforce mythology, but that doesn't mean it's incorrect. As I have argued in print, there is a difference between mythical truth and biographical truth. Myth can be defined as what we wish had happened; true biography as what really happened. More precisely, true biography is an attempt at a careful approximation of what a historical figure was like, in the days he lived. The function of a real biographer, then, is to capture biographical truth, not mythical truth.

STOVER: Would you say that biography is a function of Western society, of Western culture, or is it pretty much worldwide?

OATES: I really think that, apart from the Pueblo Indian

culture of the American Southwest, we would be hard put to isolate very many cultures throughout the course of humankind that did not, in one way or another, celebrate the heroics of exceptional people: exceptional artists, exceptional leaders, exceptional individuals of whatever creed, color, or sex. I think of the mythologies of ancient Greece that celebrated the exploits of godlike people. I think, too, of the amount of biographical attention given to Mao Tse-tung in China. Although that serves as a function of propaganda, it nevertheless indicates the value that people place upon individuals who are extraordinary. So I think that the yearn and yen for biography is a universal human trait. We want to know about how people like ourselves are born and then excel, have identity crises, work their way through them; how they may flub and fail and yet somehow work their way through to a successful conclusion. I think biography is a universal art form, in all cultures.

STOVER: Are certain biographical types more popular than others? Are there some biographies that, we might say, sell well?

OATES: There are a lot of very good biographies, unfortunately, that have never sold well. I think the best biography is a beautifully written work, distinguished for its literary excellence. Biography is, after all, a form of literature and should always be regarded as such. I think people are more apt to read a well-written biography that attempts to bring its subject to life in the context of the times than to read a dull, pedantic, fact-laden biography. One of the problems we have today is that our biographies tend toward these monstrous tomes nine hundred to one thousand pages long or even four or five volumes. We seem to be returning to the old biographical tradition of nineteenth-century Britain in which everything is put in. It's what Gore Vidal calls the "trash basket approach" to biography—where you don't leave out a thing. A succinctly, beautifully written biography is one that humanizes the subject, in which the biographer himself is careful to keep himself out, not using the "I," not strutting around giving a pompous, academic lecture on the subject, but trying to bring the subject to life much as a novelist might do.

Biographers and novelists deal with the same thing: human life and the re-creation of life. I think that's the kind of biography that sells well. It's what Justin Kaplan said is truly "literary" biography. Unfortunately, the term literary biography today is a loose catchall that refers to biographies of literary figures. But Kaplan has made a case that literary biography ought to be a much broader genre to refer to all biography that is literate, exceptionally well written, and deeply humanistic in its approach and brings back to life a human being in the context of the time.

STOVER: Are there any personality types that you think make a biography more popular or readable, owing to the nature of the subject?

OATES: It's difficult to write a very appealing, exciting biography about an absolute bore. So one has to be careful, I think, if you're out to write a biography that will have real appeal to a broad, literate audience. You want to write about somebody who had a lively personality and did something besides lie around in a room all day long. That aside, much depends on the biographer. I have read biographies of some of the most exciting people in the world that were as dull as ditchwater, mainly because the biographers were not artists and were themselves simply dull. I think that a gifted biographer with a gifted pen can find something universal, something exciting, something truly appealing, a genuine drama, in almost any kind of life. Although you might not want to write about somebody who just lay around all the time, a good biographer could do a splendid "life" of Emily Brontë, who did almost precisely that. Her fantasy or creative life, though, was spectacular. It depends on the biographer to make a life appealing, to find those hidden currents, those tensions within a life, those failures balanced off with accomplishments, that will make it appealing.

STOVER: What are some of the different ways a biographer might approach his subject to get across some of these ideas? Are there different ways of analyzing one's subject or writing about it that would make a difference in how the book turns out?

OATES: I tend to be a little doctrinaire about this. I maintain that the best biography, true biography, is a storytelling art and that the biographer has to tell a life story from beginning to end. In that sense, an essay approach to a life is anathema. I think you could do a fine biographical study, an essay on Andrew Jackson or one on Gore Vidal or Norman Mailer or one on Leonard Bernstein, once he's dead—once all three are dead—and do a nice study that analyzes their contributions and what they did. But I wouldn't call it biography. True biography, I repeat, is a storytelling art whose function is to re-create a human life, to make it live, to make it sparkle on the written page. That's why I think the overt psychoanalytic approach is antithetical to good biographical writing. It is a form in which the author himself occupies central stage and simply analyzes a dead figure. He just analyzes a name. It's the author showing off; it's the author making statements on top of a dead man or woman's casket and making no effort whatever to bring that person to life in a historical context through scene painting, interpersonal relationships, and dramatic narrative sweep. These techniques, so essential to good biography, can't be found in psychoanalytic writing.

STOVER: But can you incorporate a psychoanalytic understanding of your subject within the confines of a "good" biography?

OATES: Let me approach the question this way. We have all, in this age of psychology, learned an enormous amount from that discipline. Every good biographer uses psychological insight. One has to do that to have any kind of perception and insight into one's character. It's one thing to have psychological insight, to have learned a great deal from the disciplines of psychology and psychoanalysis about human behavior. But it's another thing to write like those people, and I submit that we should never succumb to writing like those people. If somebody wants to write using an overtly psychoanalytic style, let it be called what it is—a psychoanalytic study of a human life. But it's not biography. I think there are some standards about what biography is, just as there are about fiction. But I'm not just casting psychoanalysis out the window, not by any means. I think that any biographer must read psychoanalysis and must read psychology. But most of all he must draw on his or her own experiences and put all those together to come up with some insight into his character.

STOVER: As a biographer, you should draw on the facts of the person's life, and then perhaps this would bring you to some conclusions about the person's psyche, but you're not simply writing a scientific report——

OATES: Absolutely. I can name any number of good scenes from good biographies that convey all the psychological insights that an overtly written psychoanalytical paper published in a psychoanalytical journal could do. But in biography it's done with art and subtlety in which you don't have a sense of being lectured to. It's what Wayne Booth called the "hidden author." What the true biographer strives to do is to keep himself or herself out of the story, yet manipulate the material to present your insights and your understanding of the way the character emerged, developed, what the character became. You suggest it, you hint at it, you use Hemingway's power of suggestion through scenes and interpersonal relationships to get across your perception of the character. And all of that, of course, requires cogent psychological insights.

STOVER: You mentioned that biographical studies could be written about people who are still alive but that we have to wait until they are dead before real biographies can be done of them. Can you not write a biography of someone who is still alive?

OATES: I don't think so. I think we have to differentiate between the profile, the kind of thing that appears in the *New Yorker*, and real biography. Biography may be defined as an account of a person's life from birth to death. And we have to have access to private papers, letters, and the like to produce a biography. Most people still living are not going to surrender those. So there's a real difference between doing a profile of a still-living person and writing a biography of a person who is dead and on whom you can gain some information, find some letters or journals or diaries kept by them. That is the major difference.

Biography becomes easier, I think, when you write about longer-dead historical figures. You don't encounter problems with family, problems with lawsuits, problems with trying to get access to letters and archival materials. I could tell you stories all day about the differences in writing about Martin Luther King, Jr., which I just finished, and writing about Abraham Lincoln. Writing about the man one hundred years dead was by far the easier of the two projects.

STOVER: We talked earlier about biography reconstructing the past, and you're dealing with Abraham Lincoln, a nineteenth-century figure—do you have to learn more about that time period than that of Martin Luther King, Jr., who was alive in your lifetime?

OATES: We don't have the historical perspective on King, of course, that we do on Lincoln. On the other hand, we don't have the historical baggage, either. I don't have to work my way through twenty-five different interpretations of the man and one hundred very bad biographies to try to get some sense of what I ought to say about him. There is a mixed blessing in writing about a recently dead figure from the viewpoint of historical perspective. I realized that when I was doing King. I was going to be the first major biographer of the man, and mine was going to be the first major biography. Other biographers would play off my work for quite a number of years, and I realized what a responsibility I had. In a sense, I staked out the rules of the game. I decided what was important to write about and what was not. I decided that this needs to be stressed and this does not. As the biographer of Lincoln, I remember thinking when I read all those multitudes of Lincoln biographies, gee, those guys and women, they staked out the rules of the game, and I'm obliged, because of that extant body of literature, to play off the themes they stressed, themes they incorporated. I had to deal with the problems they raised, some of which they solved, some of which they created. Now with King, *I* was raising the questions, and I found it refreshing and extraordinarily creative.

STOVER: I would think that in a sense you're the first person to begin reconstructing that part of the past. That is to say, in the eighties we are now reconstructing various parts of the sixties.

OATES: Right. I am, in a sense, a pioneer, a biographical pioneer of Martin Luther King and the civil-rights movement. So in that sense I occupy a position that is comparable to what William Herndon occupied with respect to Lincoln biography. Except that I am not a drunkard, and I am not interested in perpetuating myths, as Herndon was. I hope that I can save King from some of the mythmaking that befell Lincoln.

STOVER: In this pioneer role, did you find that you faced any particular moral dilemmas in what you wrote about him or how you wrote? Have you found that in the other biographies?

OATES: At some point you always face a problem, and I guess it's a moral dilemma, of what you are going to do if you find warts, what you are going to do if you find rather unseemly aspects of a person's private life that might reflect badly on the person's public life. I ran into that with Abraham Lincoln. Here was a fellow who never got along with his father, scarcely ever talked about his mother, was indeed and in fact ashamed of his frontier origins. This was something that had never been stressed in the biographical literature, but it was something that the documentary evidence strongly suggested. So I had to deal with that as a moral problem: Did I want to bring in the unhappy side of Lincoln's private life? Did I want readers to know that he did not get along with his father, did not invite his father to his wedding and did not attend his father's funeral? But I reasoned that this was something that needed to be shown—that we biographers are realists as well, and we take the whole life, personal and private. You cannot understand the public life of an individual without understanding the private life. Private and public lives are a continuum, just like past and present.

With Martin Luther King I faced a much more profoundly difficult dilemma because King, to put it bluntly, was guilty of sexual indiscretions. I found that out to where there could not be any doubt. Now, does this belong in a biography of Martin Luther King, or does it not? I decided that it did but that it had to be dealt with in a very moral way. I think I dealt with it that way, and those who have read the book agree that I have. The way I tried to deal with this moral problem was to depict his indiscretion—what King called a shortcoming, a fault, a sin of his—within the context of his life. He felt prodigiously guilty about what he did. I showed that. He felt that maybe it was a way that God was punishing him for some other shortcomings he had. I wanted to show it that way, too. Most of all, I wanted to show that this was an awful price that King paid for being made into a messiah, a Jesus of his day, for being made into an angel and having a halo put over his head. He never could live up to that image. I think that when people are forced to live up to an impeccable public image like that they are more inclined to fall into trouble in their private lives. So when you write about the kinds of people I write about, extremely driven, messianic individuals caught up in tempestuous times that deal with fundamental social problems, then you are forced to deal with those moral questions.

STOVER: How do you decide whom you are going to write about? You have mentioned that you are dealing with these very driven people—is that why you chose to write about them? How does a biographer choose his or her subject?

OATES: In some way or another I think a biographer chooses to write about a figure that he or she has some rapport with; there is something that draws you to them. There is something about them that is also about you. I am not suggesting that I am an abolitionist revolutionary like John Brown or a slave rebel like Nat Turner, but I could find something about me in them. When I elected to write about John Brown, in the 1960s, I did so mainly because what John Brown dealt with still had not been resolved. I was writing on John Brown when Martin Luther King was assassinated. When that happened—as I sat horrified before my television set, listening to the haunting highlights of Martin Luther King's best speeches that grim April day in 1968 and looking at those unforgettable scenes in Memphis—I was writing the Harper's Ferry section of *John Brown*. I said, I'm writing about current events. Past and present are indeed a continuum. I had been involved in the civil-rights movement in 1961, which was what led me to John Brown. John Brown led me to Nat Turner, Nat Turner to Abraham Lincoln, Lincoln all the way back around to Martin Luther King, whose death had haunted me when I was writing about John Brown. That's the way we make our connections. I went through the 1960s battle-scarred, and I can guarantee you that's one reason I chose to write about these gentlemen. I hung those lives around the central theme of the haunting paradox of the existence of slavery in a country based on the noble ideals of the Declaration of Independence. You know, I'm a passionate, driven man myself, and somewhat of an idealist—so were all four of them.

STOVER: So the people you chose to write about were very prominent. Are most people chosen for that reason? For example, there are not very many biographies of women. Is there a particular reason for that?

OATES: Let me deal with one part of that question first. You don't have to write about a prominent figure to write a good biography. There are many excellent biographies about local people, about people who did not operate on a national or international stage. I think almost any human life is worthy of writing about if you can get the records. That's one of the problems in writing biography. You have to have letters and diaries and journals. Or at least you have to be writing about somebody you can conduct oral interviews about to gather the necessary information that enables you to put together a biography. You've got to know something about your subject's personal life as well as what he may have done. So it's rather impossible to write a biography of an American slave. It is virtually impossible to write a biography of an ordinary American housewife of the 1830s and 1840s because she lived in a form of slavery as well. You have to write about people who had enough sense of themselves to leave behind this kind of documentary record that I just described, or whose peers and colleagues or enemies and friends thought enough of them that they preserved the letters that the subjects themselves wrote. I've had people approach me about this and insist that biography is, by nature, elitist. I don't like that word. I'm simply saying that it has to be about people who, wherever they operated, whether on a local stage, a national stage, or an international stage, had to do something to leave behind a written record that we can use. Martin Luther King left behind another kind of record. He had an enormous impact on the people who worked with him. He changed their lives. They've never gotten over his assassination. Once you can get them to talk and reminisce about those years not too long gone, then that's another form of record that is fantastic and indispensable.

STOVER: So you might either write a story about a well-known historical figure or you can take someone less well known, write a good story about that person, and make him or her a well-known historical figure?

OATES: Exactly. You find the universal in any life, and you have something that will appeal to people and that they will read about. Now, as far as women are concerned, you ask why are there so few biographies of women. Why are there so few women biographers? That's the real question. Unfortunately, my female colleagues in the disciplines of the humanities, for some reason, are not really turning to biography. There are not any epic biographies, great storytelling biographies in the great storytelling tradition, about some of the leading women of the nineteenth century. Elizabeth Cady Stanton, Susan B. Anthony, Margaret Fuller all lack substantial, literary biographies. There are small studies about them, there are collections of their letters, there is statistical stuff done on them. Maybe this is the rub: my female colleagues are attempting to prove their credentials, their academic credentials. Many of them, perhaps most of them, are working in universities and facing tenure committees. It's unfortunate that the field of history is tending off toward recondite social science. And biography in history departments has, I'm afraid, fallen into disrepute. As a consequence, my female colleagues in the discipline of history are not writing biographies. They have got to face these tenure committees, so they're writing these abstruse, statistical, sociological treatises about women—groups of them, not individuals. They could put you to sleep. They are not being very widely read, and they're not going to be. I hope that once women are accepted in the academic disciplines, once they don't have to prove themselves any more to a male-dominated world, then women with those gifted pens will set themselves loose on biographical subjects and produce brilliant biographies.

The second problem about women is that, apart from the women I mentioned a moment ago, the leaders of the women's rights movement of the nineteenth century, it's probably a comment on American culture that there are so few biographies, even by men, about nineteenth-century women. Women, because they lived in a form of servitude in the Victorian age, were not allowed to get out and do enough to merit biographical attention. Many of them—I'm talking about ordinary American women—did not have enough sense of themselves to save their letters. Nor did their husbands or anyone else. Maybe their friends saved them, and they got tossed out. No archives were interested. There are still plenty of women to write about in the nineteenth century, but there will never be as many biographies about women in that century as about men because it was a male-dominated time. But Jean Strouse's biography of Alice James shows you that a good biography can be done about a human being who was overshadowed by the brilliant men in her family. We may have a whole lot of Alice Jameses out there to be written about.

STOVER: Any closing thoughts?

OATES: I think that pretty much summarizes my views on biography as I've studied and practiced the form. Biography has changed my life. Living through four other human lives besides my own has enriched me immeasurably as a writer and as a human being. I may have re-created Martin Luther King's life, but he changed mine.

Geoffrey Rips with Jean Strouse

Rips: What led you to write a biography of Alice James rather than a history of late-nineteenth-century women and neurasthenia?

Strouse: I think it's more interesting to approach an understanding of nineteenth-century history and something like neurasthenia through someone's life. It opens up avenues into the past that reading straight history doesn't do. You get windows on more aspects of what happened by having to think about what life was like for an individual. In the process of looking at Alice James's life, I learned a great many things about neurasthenia that might not have been available to me otherwise. Rather than looking at the large movements of history or using the "winds of change" kind of approach, the approach to history through an individual's life is for me the most suggestive about what was really going on. This is how I feel as both a writer and a reader.

Rips: Choosing somebody like Alice James has its advantages because so much has been written by and about members of her family and so much of their correspondence still exists. Did you choose that life to illuminate other lives that were not so extensively chronicled?

Strouse: Well, yes and no. I think it's the specificity of her life that is interesting, rather than her role as a representative. She happens to be representative of a number of things, but that's not why I originally thought she was interesting. That was secondary; it concerned what went on around her.

Looking at an obscure life—as many social historians are doing these days—really does show you kinds of things very different from what you would find looking at lives that have been in the limelight, both while they are being lived and afterwards through biographers and historians. It approximates more closely what ordinary daily life was like, and that's what we don't know very much about. Social historians try to find out with demographic records and statistical analyses.

Biography is another approach. Quite risky and tricky. I spent five years answering the question, "Why are you doing this?" It was not obvious that Alice James was interesting. She really did seem like a footnote to the lives of famous men. And yet the sorts of people that Henry James wrote about were very much like his sister.

With Alice James I was lucky. Because her family was famous, many documents were saved. Because there was a record of her life, I could get to know her. If someone wanted to look at the life of an ordinary anonymous nineteenth-century American woman, it simply couldn't be done. If she had kept diaries and letters all her life and if those had been saved and passed on through the next four generations, it might be possible. But then she wouldn't have been ordinary. She would have had to be someone like Harriet Beecher Stowe. So this was an extraordinary avenue for me. I wrote a piece about doing this kind of biography in *Studies in Biography*. It was called "Semi-Private Lives." It was about this sort of twilight zone occupied by Alice James and others who were related to, by either marriage or birth, somebody famous. It throws fascinating light in two directions: both on the life of fame and glitter, in which people had a sense that they were really influencing history, and on that other, more private realm, which is much harder to see. Part of what I liked about doing this was that window on two worlds.

Alice certainly suffered from living in that twilight zone. She measured herself against those rather grand creatures who were her brothers, as well she might. She felt that she should have done something to measure up to what they did and certainly never managed to. I don't think she was a genius, by any means, and the fact that she wasn't, while it seems all right to us, was disturbing to her.

RIPS: I thought that the end of your book was a little ambiguous in that it seemed to be saying that she was a great writer or, at least, would have been had she not suffered so much. That's almost what she accused William James of saying about her. Were you saying that she deserved a biography as a writer?

STROUSE: I don't think I was. No. There were flashes of brilliance in that diary, but it's not the work of a fine writer. She was, at times, extremely mannered. It would be foolish to say that she might have written the great nineteenth-century American novel. I think she's interesting as a mind, sometimes extremely fine and sometimes rather mundane. It was much more her character than her writing that I was interested in. The main evidence I had about her, however, was from the diaries and letters. So I had to make a great deal out of them.

RIPS: I was going to ask you why there have been so few biographies about women, but I'd rather ask what the importance is of writing a biography about a woman like Alice James rather than about George Sand.

STROUSE: That's sort of what we've been talking about, and I think it's a more interesting question. H. G. Wells said, "History is the chronicles of wars and kings." Most people who waged wars and became monarchs were men (though there have been plenty of biographies of Joan of Arc and the English queens)—so if you see history that way, you see it through the lives of great men. If you expand the idea of history, however, you include people like Jane Austen, George Sand, George Eliot, Marie Curie, and Florence Nightingale (as well as men who weren't generals or kings), and there are plenty of biographies of them. Now, of course, women are doing more of the things that make people famous—and people like me are writing books about women who didn't do anything—so the whole field is changing.

Alice James appealed to me partly because of what I was saying about a window on two worlds. Also, I was quite interested in the kinds of psychological troubles she had. She died just three years before Freud published his "Studies on Hysteria"—and she was a classic hysteric. She was also diagnosed "neurasthenic," and the struggles of a great many upper- and middle-class men and women with neurasthenia in the late nineteenth century make up an important chapter in American social history. These illnesses were experienced individually, but they were so widespread as to become a social phenomenon. Also, you can't entirely separate psychological and social experience. For instance, there were a great many more women than men in Massachusetts in the last decades of the nineteenth century, as a result of the Civil War and the movement west. That social fact definitely influenced how New England women had to live. Some of them went to work instead of getting married; some set up house together in what was called a "Boston marriage." In the past, as in the present, it's interesting to look at how social facts and events affect people's particular, private lives.

RIPS: And Alice?

STROUSE: Alice cannot be seen simply as a victim of social forces, since many other women managed to cope quite well in the same circumstances. Alice just caved in, becoming a professional invalid. That's what I meant about the interaction of public and private, because whatever "explanations" there are about Alice lie deep within her family and her personality. That's another thing that sparked my interest in her: the opportunity to look at how individuals in a family respond to each other and to some of the same dynamics in each making his or her own way. Sartre said something about neurosis being an original solution the child invents on the point of stifling to death. In that sense, Alice's illness was her creation. It is interesting not in the way that Henry's great novels are or William's philosophy and psychology—but in showing how somebody works and functions under stress to define his or her own life's sense and meaning.

RIPS: That leads to an important question: Has the incorporation of psychoanalytic theory in the writing of biography been successful?

STROUSE: Not very often. I think it's extremely difficult to do well because the language of most psychoanalytic thinking is so off-putting for people who aren't already initiated. People who know it find it very hard not to use it. So it becomes very difficult to combine that knowledge with a more literary sensibility—though it's necessary if you are going to write a biography that will appeal to anyone outside the psychoanalytic profession. It hasn't been done very often. Leon Edel does it in his biography of Henry James, and I think several other writers who haven't necessarily been touted as psychologically sophisticated do it because they have a marvelous sense of what makes people tick.

RIPS: I thought that's what you were doing in *Alice James*. You seemed to be probing the way Henry James probes in his novels and the way the protean psychologists of that time were probing without really applying a theory to their subject.

STROUSE: Thanks. That's just what I was trying to do. Nobody lives his or her life in a way that's reducible to a theory. Henry's novels show people's internal conflicts and the growth of perception in ways that are not at all visible until you get deeply into the story, and then you begin to see—with a character—how things work and what's going on. That was what I was trying to do: to illuminate aspects of a life from the inside.

The sort of evidence you have in writing a biography is not the same evidence you would have if you were a psychoanalyst dealing with a live patient. You can't ask direct questions. You just have to go with what's there. You can't see deep into intrapsychic conflicts—you can only glimpse whatever evidence leaks out. In the nineteenth century people let a great deal leak out because they weren't as self-conscious as we are. The evidence lies in letters, diaries, work themes, dreams—whatever got verbally reported—and it shows you a lot about what was going on between people. There is more reliable evidence about that—you can see people's interactions in their letters to each other, for instance—than there is about deep unconscious motivations.

RIPS: Do you think recent technology has affected modern biography?

STROUSE: The idea of being able to store information technologically seems to be extremely interesting and yet problematic. I have been thinking about getting a word processor. With *Alice James* what I had to do was make indexes of every letter I collected so that I would have cross references for the sender, the receiver, and the content. I had lists so

that if a letter mentioned Oliver Wendell Holmes, for instance, I could later go to the lists to find the right letters. It
meant that I had to reread all the material fairly often to
make the index. With all that rereading, the material soaks
into your mind. I can quote whole passages of letters, and I
haven't read those things in four years. There's something
about immediate physical contact with the material that—and
this is very old-fashioned of me—might be lost if it were just
in a data bank. Having to familiarize yourself with it that way,
it enters your own character by osmosis as more than a piece
of information. Seeing all that material in those people's
handwriting every time you have to look it up, rather than
seeing it on a screen, makes a big difference. You get a sense
of personality from handwriting. When Henry talks about
his cousin Minny Temple, you know how the whole letter
feels and not just one particular passage. There's something
important about that. It has to do with your feeling for the
people you write about.

RIPS: And the reader must sense that as well?

STROUSE: I think biography works best when the biographer gives almost a fictional life to a character. You can
have all the information in the world, but if there somehow
hasn't been that extra leap to make a reader feel involved in
the life of the subject and interested in it, then the homework
doesn't matter. It dies on the page. The biography of E. M.
Forster, by Philip N. Furbank, did that in an amazing way
because it wasn't a very interesting life. Not much happened
to Forster. And yet the sensibility that Furbank brought to
his life makes him vivid in a rare and fascinating way.

I had a problem with Alice James in that I didn't like her
a lot of the time. In fact, I experienced a sort of crisis toward
the halfway point in writing because I really got quite furious
at her and frustrated with her, and I got stuck. I knew how
the story was going to end, and I didn't want it to end that
way. I realized that I'd gotten more involved in it than I'd
realized and that she'd somehow done something to me that
I hadn't been aware of. I had to leave it and come back a
month later, feeling that I had accepted what was going to

happen to her. I didn't have to agree with it; I didn't have to identify with it; I didn't have to like it. I had to understand it. It was a crucial moment for me.

I think some sort of emotional connection has to be made for the biography to be vivid, for the person to come to life. Then the historical period that person inhabits comes to life too.

But I don't want to generalize about what works and what doesn't. It must be different for each subject. Next time I may try something very different—probably a man and probably somebody famous.

Bibliography

Editor's note: The following bibliography primarily contains authors and works cited in the papers included in this volume. The bibliography was expanded to include additional works of some authors to assist the reader in further study.

Aaron, Daniel, ed. *Studies in Biography*. Cambridge, Mass.: Harvard University Press, 1978.

Abzug, Robert H. *Passionate Liberator: Theodore Dwight Weld & the Dilemma of Reform*. New York: Oxford University Press, 1980.

Alexander, Franz. *History of Psychiatry*. New York: Harper & Row, 1966.

Altick, Richard. *Lives and Letters: A History of Literary Biographies in England and America*. New York: Knopf, 1965.

Bell, Eric T. *Men of Mathematics*. New York: Simon and Schuster, 1937.

Berger, Peter L. *The Sacred Canopy: Elements of a Sociological Theory of Religion*. Garden City, N.Y.: Doubleday, 1967.

———— and Thomas Luckmann. *The Social Construction of Reality: A Treastise in the Sociology of Knowledge*. Garden City, N.Y.: Doubleday, 1966.

Beveridge, Albert J. *The Life of John Marshall*. 4 vols. Boston and New York: Houghton Mifflin, 1916–19.

Boswell, James. *The Life of Samuel Johnson*. London: H. Baldwin, 1791; edited by R. W. Chapman as *Boswell's Life of Johnson*. London: Oxford University Press, 1953.

Bowen, Catherine Drinker. *Adventures of a Biographer*. Boston: Little, Brown, 1959.

————. *Biography: The Craft and the Calling*. Boston: Little, Brown, 1968.

————. *Yankee from Olympus*. Boston: Little, Brown, 1944.

Bradford, Gamaliel. *American Portraits, 1875–1900*. Boston and New York: Houghton Mifflin, 1922.

————. *Biography and the Human Heart*. Boston and New York: Houghton Mifflin, 1932.

————. *Confederate Portraits*. Boston and New York: Houghton Mifflin, 1914.

———. *Damaged Souls*. Boston and New York: Houghton Mifflin, 1923.

———. *Portraits of American Women*. Boston and New York: Houghton Mifflin, 1919.

———. *Union Portraits*. Boston and New York: Houghton Mifflin, 1916.

Carlson, Elof Axel, ed. *Hermann J. Muller, 1890–1967*. Albany: State University of New York Press, 1973.

Churchill, Winston S. *Marlborough, His Life and Times*. 2 vols. London: Harrap, 1947.

Clark, Ronald. *Freud: The Man and the Cause*. New York: Random House, 1980.

Clifford, James L. *Biography as an Art*. Oxford: Oxford University Press, 1962.

———. *From Puzzles to Portraits: Problems of a Literary Biographer*. Chapel Hill: University of North Carolina Press, 1970.

Cobb, Richard C. *Death in Paris*. Oxford and New York: Oxford University Press, 1978.

———. *Paris and Its Provinces, 1792–1802*. London and New York: Oxford University Press, 1975.

Dugger, Ronald. *The Politician*. New York: Norton, 1982.

Edel, Leon. "The Figure under the Carpet." In Marc Pachter, ed. *Telling Lives: The Biographer's Art*, pp. 16–34. Washington, D.C.: New Republic Books, 1979; reprint, Philadelphia: University of Pennsylvania Press, 1981.

———. *Henry James*. 5 vols. Philadelphia: Lippincott, 1953–72.

———. *Literary Biography*. London: R. Hart-Davis, 1957.

Ellmann, Richard. *Literary Biography*. Oxford: Clarendon Press, 1971.

Erikson, Erik H. *Gandhi's Truth: On the Origins of Militant Nonviolence*. New York: Norton, 1969.

———. *Young Man Luther*. New York: Norton, 1958.

Freeman, Douglas Southall. *George Washington: A Biography*. 7 vols. New York: Scribner's, 1948–57.

———. *R. E. Lee: A Biography*. 4 vols. New York: Scribner's, 1934–35.

Freud, Sigmund. *Autobiographical Study*. Translated by James Strachey. New York: Norton, 1925.

———. *Leonardo da Vinci: A Psychosexual Study of an Infantile Reminiscence*. Translated by A. A. Brill. New York: Moffat, Yard and Norton, 1935.

———, and William C. Bullitt. *Thomas Woodrow Wilson, Twenty-eighth*

President of the United States: A Psychological Study. Boston: Houghton Mifflin, 1967.

Friedson, Anthony M., ed. *New Directions in Biography*. Honolulu: University of Hawaii Press, 1981.

Froude, James Anthony. *Thomas Carlyle: A History of the First Forty Years of His Life, 1795–1835* and *Thomas Carlyle: A History of His Life in London, 1834–1881*. 4 vols. London: Longmans, Green, 1882, 1884. Abridged and edited by John Clubbe as *Froude's Life of Carlyle*. Columbus: Ohio State University Press, 1979.

Furbank, Philip N. *E. M. Forster: A Life*. London: Secker and Warburg, 1977. First American edition, New York: Harcourt Brace Jovanovich, 1978.

Garraty, John A. *The Nature of Biography*. London: J. Cape, 1958.

George, Alexander L., and Juliette L. George. *Woodrow Wilson and Colonel House: A Personality Study*. New York: John Day, 1956.

Graves, Robert. *I, Claudius*. New York: H. Smith and R. Haas, 1934.

James, Marquis. *Andrew Jackson: Portrait of a President*. Indianapolis, Ind., and New York: Bobbs-Merrill, 1937.

———. *The Raven: A Biography of Sam Houston*. Indianapolis, Ind.: Bobbs-Merrill, 1929.

Jones, Ernest. *The Life and Work of Sigmund Freud*. 3 vols. New York: Basic Books, 1953–57.

Kaplan, Justin. *Lincoln Steffens: A Biography*. New York: Simon and Schuster, 1974.

———. *Mr. Clemens and Mark Twain: A Biography*. New York: Simon and Schuster, 1966.

———. "The Naked Self and Other Problems." In Marc Pachter, ed. *Telling Lives: The Biographer's Art*, pp. 36–55. Washington, D.C.: New Republic Books, 1979; reprint, Philadelphia: University of Pennsylvania Press, 1981.

———. *Walt Whitman: A Life*. New York: Simon and Schuster, 1980.

Kearns, Doris. *Lyndon Johnson & the American Dream*. New York: Harper & Row, 1976.

Kendall, Paul Murray. *The Art of Biography*. New York: Norton, 1965.

———. *Louis XI: The Universal Spider*. New York: Norton, 1970.

———. *Richard the Third*. New York: Norton, 1956.

Kevles, Daniel J. *The Physicists: The History of a Scientific Community*. New York: Knopf, 1978.

Kraus, Michael. *A History of American History*. New York: Farrar and Rinehart, 1937.

Light, Donald. *Becoming Psychiatrists: The Professional Transformation of Self.* New York: Norton, 1980.

Malone, Dumas. *Jefferson and His Time.* 6 vols. Boston: Little, Brown, 1948–81.

Mariani, Paul. *William Carlos Williams: A New World Naked.* New York: McGraw-Hill, 1981.

Maurois, André. *Aspects of Biography.* New York: D. Appleton, 1930.

Mattingly, Garrett. *The Armada.* Boston: Houghton Mifflin, 1959.

Mitford, Nancy. *Zelda: A Biography.* New York: Harper & Row, 1970.

Nehls, Edward, ed. *D. H. Lawrence: A Composite Biography.* Madison: University of Wisconsin Press, 1957–59.

Nemerov, Howard. *The Collected Poems of Howard Nemerov.* Chicago: University of Chicago Press, 1977.

Nutting, Anthony. *Lawrence of Arabia: The Man and the Motive.* New York: Potter, 1961.

Oates, Stephen B. *The Fires of Jubilee: Nat Turner's Fierce Rebellion.* New York: Harper & Row, 1975.

———. *Let the Trumpet Sound: The Life of Martin Luther King, Jr.* New York: Harper & Row, 1982.

———. *To Purge This Land with Blood: A Biography of John Brown.* New York: Harper & Row, 1970.

———. *With Malice toward None: The Life of Abraham Lincoln.* New York: Harper & Row, 1977.

Pachter, Marc. ed. *Telling Lives: The Biographer's Art.* Washington, D.C.: New Republic Books, 1979; reprint, Philadelphia: University of Pennsylvania Press, 1981.

Perry, Helen Swick. *Psychiatrist of America: The Life of Harry Stack Sullivan.* Cambridge, Mass.: Harvard University Press, Belknap Press, 1982.

Plutarch. *Plutarch's Lives.* Translated by Bernadotte Perrin. 11 vols. Cambridge, Mass.: Harvard University Press, 1955–62.

Pogue, Forrest C. *George C. Marshall.* New York: Viking, 1963.

Rudé, George F. *The Crowd in History.* New York: Wiley, 1964.

Sachs, Hanns. *Freud, Master & Friend.* Cambridge, Mass.: Harvard University Press, 1945.

Sandoz, Mari. *Crazy Horse.* New York: Knopf, 1942.

———. *Old Jules.* Boston: Little, Brown, 1935.

Schorer, Mark. *Sinclair Lewis: An American Life.* New York: McGraw-Hill, 1961.

Shotwell, James Thomson. *The History of History.* New York: Columbia University Press, 1939.

Steel, Ronald. *Walter Lippmann and the American Century.* Boston: Little, Brown, 1980.

Strachey, Giles Lytton. *Biographical Essays.* New York: Harcourt, Brace, 1949.

―――. *Books and Characters.* New York: Harcourt, Brace, 1922.

―――. *Characters and Commentaries.* New York: Harcourt, Brace, 1933.

―――. *Eminent Victorians.* London: Chatto & Windus, 1918.

―――. *Portraits in Miniature.* New York: Harcourt, Brace, 1931.

―――. *Queen Victoria.* New York: Harcourt, Brace, 1921.

Strouse, Jean. *Alice James: A Biography.* Boston: Houghton Mifflin, 1980.

Suetonius, Tranquillus. *Suetonius.* Translated by J. C. Rolfe. 2 vols. Cambridge, Mass.: Harvard University Press, 1950.

Sulloway, Frank. *Freud: Biologist of the Mind.* New York: Basic Books, 1975.

Thomas, Benjamin P. *Theodore Weld: Crusader for Freedom.* New Brunswick, N.J.: Rutgers University Press, 1950.

Troyat, Henri. *Tolstoy.* Garden City, N.Y.: Doubleday, 1967.

Tuchman, Barbara W. "Biography as Prism of History." In Marc Pachter, ed. *Telling Lives: The Biographer's Art,* pp. 132–47. Washington, D.C.: New Republic Press, 1979; reprint, Philadelphia: University of Pennsylvania Press, 1981.

―――. *A Distant Mirror: The Calamitous Fourteenth Century.* New York: Macmillan, 1966.

―――. *The Proud Tower: A Portrait of the World before the War.* New York: Macmillan, 1966.

Vandiver, Frank. *Black Jack: The Life and Times of John J. Pershing.* 2 vols. College Station: Texas A&M University Press, 1977.

―――. *Mighty Stonewall.* New York: McGraw-Hill, 1957.

Van Loon, Hendrik Willem. *Van Loon's Lives.* New York: Simon and Schuster, 1942.

Wheeler-Bennett, John. *Wooden Titan: Hindenburg in Twenty Years of German History, 1914–1934.* New York: Morrow, 1936.

White, Robert W. *Lives in Progress: A Study in the Natural Growth of Personality.* New York: Dryden, 1952.

Williams, T. Harry. *Huey Long.* Oxford: Clarendon Press, 1967.

―――. *Lincoln and His Generals.* New York: Knopf, 1952.

―――. *P. T. G. Beauregard: Napoleon in Gray.* Baton Rouge: Louisiana State University Press, 1960.

Winslow, Donald J. *Life-Writing: A Glossary of Terms in Biography,*

Autobiography, and Related Forms. Honolulu: University of Hawaii Press, 1980.

Yeats, William Butler. *The Collected Poems of W. B. Yeats*. New York: Macmillan, 1933.

Contributors

ROBERT H. ABZUG is assistant professor of History at the University of Texas at Austin. He was educated at Harvard University (B.A.) and the University of California, Berkeley (Ph.D.). His *Passionate Liberator: Theodore Dwight Weld & the Dilemma of Reform* was the Oxford University Press's nominee for the Frederick Jackson Turner Prize in 1980. He is currently working on *Cosmos Crumbling: Antebellum Reform and the Search for Sacred Connection* and is collecting material for a research project concerning American reactions to Nazi genocide during and after World War II.

JOE HOLLEY is editor of the *Texas Observer*. He is former staff member of the Texas Committee for the Humanities and past editor of the *Texas Humanist*. He has contributed articles and essays on a wide range of topics to various publications, including the *Dallas Times Herald*, *Texas Monthly*, and the *Texas Observer*. He has taught in the Dallas Community College District. He received the M.A. degree in English from the University of Texas at Austin and the M.S. degree from Columbia University School of Journalism.

STEPHEN B. OATES is professor of History and adjunct professor of English at the University of Massachusetts, Amherst. He received the B.A., M.A., and Ph.D. degrees from the University of Texas at Austin. He is best known for his civil-rights biographical quartet: *To Purge This Land with Blood: A Biography of John Brown* (1970), *The Fires of Jubilee: Nat Turner's Fierce Rebellion* (1975), *With Malice toward None: The Life of Abraham Lincoln* (1977); and *Let the Trumpet Sound: The Life of Martin Luther King, Jr.* (1982). He is the author of other books and articles on the Civil War and the American West and South. He has received fellowships from the Guggenheim Foundation and the National Endowment for the Humanities. The biography of Nat Turner was a Pulitzer Prize nominee in 1975, and the biography of Lincoln won the Christopher Award for Outstanding Literature in 1977.

GEOFFREY RIPS is associate editor of the *Texas Observer* and a former coordinator of the Freedom to Write program of the PEN

American Center in New York City. His poetry has appeared in *For Neruda, For Chile*, the *California Quarterly, Travois*, and elsewhere. His fiction has appeared in the *Oxford Literary Review* and *New Directions*, and his articles and book reviews have appeared in the *Nation, Index on Censorship*, and the *Oxford Literary Review*. He is the author of *Unamerican Activities: The Campaign against the Underground Press* (1981).

RONALD STEEL is the author of four books and many articles, essays, and book reviews. He currently is a contributing editor of the *New Republic*. His essays on United States politics and foreign policy have appeared in the *New York Times*, the *Washington Post, Harper's*, the *Atlantic, Commentary*, the *Saturday Review*, and other leading journals and newspapers. His analysis and critique of American cold war diplomacy, *Pax Americana* (1967), received the Sydney Hillman Book Award. *Walter Lippmann and the American Century* (1980) received the Bancroft Prize in American History, the National Book Critics Circle Award, the Los Angeles Times Book Award, and the Washington Monthly Book Award. Steel, who holds an M.A. degree from Harvard University, has held visiting professorships at the University of California at Los Angeles, the University of California at Irvine, the University of Texas at Austin, Rutgers University, and Wellesley College. He is a former Foreign Service officer, having served in Washington, D.C., and on Cyprus.

JEANNE HOPKINS STOVER received the B.A. degree in speech communication from Northern Illinois University. She served as press secretary for a United States congressional campaign in Wisconsin before moving to Massachusetts to become a radio news reporter. She is now broadcast editor at the University of Massachusetts, Amherst, where she produces *Commonwealth Journal*, a syndicated half-hour weekly radio interview program.

JEAN STROUSE is a general editor and book critic of *Newsweek*. She received the B.A. degree in English from Radcliffe College and has been awarded fellowships for independent study from the National Endowment for the Arts, the National Endowment for the Humanities, and the Guggenheim Memorial Foundation. She is the author of *Women and Analysis: Dialogues on Psychoanalytic Views of Femininity* (1974). Her *Alice James: A Biography* (1980) won the

Bancroft Prize in American History and Diplomacy. She resides in New York.

FRANK E. VANDIVER received the Ph.D. degree from Tulane University. He served in various capacities at Rice University from 1955 to 1979, as professor of History, chairman of the Department of History, provost and vice-president, and acting president. He has held visiting professorships at Oxford University and the United States Military Academy at West Point. He was president of North Texas State University from 1979 to 1981 and currently serves as president of Texas A&M University. A military historian and biographer, he is the author of nine books, including *Rebel Brass: The Confederate Command System* (1956), *Mighty Stonewall* (1957), *Their Tattered Flags: The Epic of the Confederacy* (1970), and *Black Jack: The Life and Times of John J. Pershing* (1977). The biography of Pershing was a finalist in the National Book Awards competition.

JAMES F. VENINGA is executive director of the Texas Committee for the Humanities. He received the B.A. degree in philosophy from Baylor University, the M.T.S. degree from Harvard Divinity School, and M.A. and Ph.D. degrees in history and religious studies from Rice University. He has held teaching positions at Middle Tennessee State University and the University of St. Thomas, Houston. He is editor of the *Texas Humanist* and serves as general editor for publications of the Texas Committee for the Humanities.

STEVEN WEILAND is executive director of the National Federation of State Humanities Councils. He was educated at the City University of New York (B.A.) and the University of Chicago (Ph.D.). He has taught English and American Studies at the University of Michigan and has served as assistant vice-president for Continuing Education and Metropolitan Affairs at the University of Cincinnati. He has held scholarly fellowships at the University of Chicago and the University of Michigan and in 1975 was Taft Fellow in Humanities and Education at the University of Cincinnati. His articles on the humanities, higher education, literature, anthropology, and psychoanalysis have appeared in various journals.

Index

99–100, 110–11; and biology, 6;
Freudian, and American psychiatry,
54; and history, 84; and interpretations of professions, 46–50, 53; and
novels, 82. *See also* biography, psychoanalytic
psychobiography, 37, 52, 82–83, 84,
89–90, 93, 94. *See also* biography,
psychoanalytic
psychohistory, 37
psychology: as biographical tool, 5, 9,
37, 40, 60, 63, 99–100, 111; and biography, 68, 76, 93, 109–10; dynamic, 6; and history, 5–6, 76; and
social science, 6; and truth, 29

reality, objective, 66–68. *See also* fate;
freedom
reminiscences, 15
research: access to materials for, 101,
105, 107, 108, 111; approaches to, 7,
84–85; discussion of, 8; and good
life-writing, 11, 30; modern techniques of, 16; oral interviews in, 105;
originality in, 17; use of data in, 4, 5
Richter, Jean Paul, 20
Rips, Geoffrey, 91–95, 107–13
Rolland, Romain, 15
Rostovtzeff, Michael I., 15
Rudé, George F.: *The Crowd in History*, 6

"sacred canopy," 66–75, 78
Sandburg, Carl, 96
Sandoz, Mari, 32
Santayana, George, 4
Schaeffer, William, 44, 49
Schorer, Mark, 11
science, 5, 6, 7, 9, 11, 24, 50
self, psychiatric, 45–50. *See also* psychoanalysis
sequence, chronological, 17, 21, 24
Shotwell, James Thomson: *History of
History*, 7
sketch, biographical, 12, 13, 52
social sciences: and biography, 5, 6, 11,
37, 96, 105–106; influence of psychology on, 6; jargon in, 7
social values, 26–27, 39, 40
society, "sacred canopy" of, 66–75, 78

sociology, 6, 49, 66, 106
Solzhenitsyn, Alexander, 15
Steel, Ronald, 26–29, 68, 91–95; *Walter
Lippmann and the American Century*,
23, 53, 69–72, 77–78, 81, 91–94
Stover, Jeanne Hopkins, 96–106
Strachey, Lytton, 9, 15, 32; *Eminent Vic-
torians*, 10, 12–13; influence of, 63;
Life of Queen Victoria, 10
Strouse, Jean, 37–41, 60, 68, 107–113;
Alice James, 23, 32, 38–40, 53, 65, 69,
72–75, 76, 81, 93, 106
"Semi-Private Lives," 109
Suetonius, 9
suggestion, power of, 32, 100
Sullivan, Harry Stack, 53–54
Sulloway, Frank: *Freud: Biologist of the
Mind*, 50–51
Sun Tzu, 14
superimposition: of author, 28, 29

Taylor, General Maxwell, 14
technology, 16, 111–12
tensions: between fate and freedom,
64–67, 75, 78; internal, 26, 99
Thomas, Benjamin: *Theodore Dwight
Weld: Crusader for Freedom*, 89
Toynbee, Arnold, 15
Troyat, Henri: *Tolstoy*, 30
Tuchman, Barbara W., 3, 30; "Biogra-
phy as a Prism of History," 12, 62,
63–64; *A Distant Mirror*, 62–63; *The
Proud Tower*, 63
Turner, Nat, 33, 35, 103–104. *See also*
Oates, Stephen B.

understanding, 19, 21, 39, 59, 60, 103,
113
universality, 12, 25, 32, 78, 97, 98, 105

values: cultural, 27, 28–29, 63–64, 66–
67; personal, 61; social, 26–27, 39,
40, 66–67
Vandiver, Frank E., 3–20; biography of
Pershing by, 59, 64, 81; biography of
Stonewall Jackson by, 19, 32; re-
sponses to, 21–41, 59, 62, 68–69, 79
Van Loon, Hendrik Willem: *Lives*, 12
Veninga, James F., 59–79